Getting Started in

HEDGE FUNDS

Books in the *Getting Started in* Series

Getting Started in Asset Allocation by Bill Bresnan and Eric P. Gelb
Getting Started in Investment Clubs by Marsha Bertrand
Getting Started in Internet Auctions by Alan Elliott
Getting Started in Stocks by Alvin D. Hall
Getting Started in Mutual Funds by Alvin D. Hall
Getting Started in Estate Planning by Kerry Hannon
Getting Started in Online Personal Finance by Brad Hill
Getting Started in 401(k) Investing by Paul Katzeff
Getting Started in Security Analysis by Peter J. Klein
Getting Started in Global Investing by Robert P. Kreitler
Getting Started in Futures, Fifth Edition by Todd Lofton
Getting Started in Financial Information by Daniel Moreau and Tracey Longo
Getting Started in Emerging Markets by Christopher Poillon
Getting Started in Technical Analysis by Jack D. Schwager
Getting Started in Real Estate Investing by Michael C. Thomsett and Jean Freestone
Getting Started in Tax-Savvy Investing by Andrew Westham and Don Korn
Getting Started in Annuities by Gordon M. Williamson
Getting Started in Bonds, Second Edition by Sharon Saltzgiver Wright
Getting Started in Retirement Planning by Ronald M. Yolles and Murray Yolles
Getting Started in Project Management by Paula Martin and Karen Tate
Getting Started in Six Sigma by Michael C. Thomsett
Getting Started in Rental Income by Michael C. Thomsett
Getting Started in REITs by Richard Imperiale
Getting Started in Property Flipping by Michael C. Thomsett
Getting Started in Fundamental Analysis by Michael C. Thomsett
Getting Started in Chart Patterns by Thomas N. Bulkowski
Getting Started in ETFs by Todd K. Lofton
Getting Started in Swing Trading by Michael C. Thomsett
Getting Started in Options, Seventh Edition by Michael C. Thomsett
Getting Started in A Financially Secure Retirement by Henry Hebeler
Getting Started in Candlestick Charting by Tina Logan
Getting Started in Forex Trading Strategies by Michael D. Archer
Getting Started in Value Investing by Charles Mizrahi
Getting Started in Currency Trading, Second Edition by Michael D. Archer
Getting Started in Options, Eighth Edition by Michael C. Thomsett
Getting Started in Rebuilding Your 401(k), Second Edition by Paul Katzeff
Getting Started in Mutual Funds, Second Edition by Alvin D. Hall

Getting Started in

HEDGE FUNDS

THIRD EDITION

From Launching a Hedge Fund to New Regulation, the Use of Leverage, and Top Manager Profiles

Daniel A. Strachman

John Wiley & Sons, Inc.

Published by John Wiley & Sons, Inc., Hoboken, New Jersey.
Published simultaneously in Canada.

For general information on our other products and services or for technical support, please contact our Customer Care Department within the United States at (800) 762-2974, outside the United States at (317) 572-3993 or fax (317) 572-4002.

Wiley also publishes its books in a variety of electronic formats. Some content that appears in print may not be available in electronic books. For more information about Wiley products, visit our web site at www.wiley.com.

Library of Congress Cataloging-in-Publication Data:

Strachman, Daniel A., 1971-

Getting started in hedge funds: from launching a hedge fund to new regulation, the use of leverage, and top manager profiles / Daniel A. Strachman. – 3rd ed.

p. cm. – (Getting started in..... ; 88)

Includes bibliographical references and index.

ISBN 978-0-470-63025-9 (pbk.); ISBN 978-1-118-01896-5 (ebk);
ISBN 978-1-118-01897-2 (ebk); ISBN 978-1-118-01898-9 (ebk)

1. Hedge funds. I. Title.

HG4530.S837 2010

332.64'524–dc22

2010023267

Printed in the United States of America

10 9 8 7 6 5 4 3 2 1

To my wife, Felice,
my daughter, Leah
and my son, Jonah

Contents

Chapter 4

Acknowledgments

The idea for the first edition of this book came to me in the mid-1990s while I was working at Cantor Fitzgerald and, as a result of a number of unique events, that book became a reality in January of 2000. Now some ten years later, Wiley is publishing a third edition.

I started working on this revision in December 2009, and over the past four or five months, I have tried to update the pages of this book to make it as relevant as possible for those interested in learning more about hedge funds and the hedge fund industry. I hope that you, the reader, find it worthwhile and, more importantly, worthy of your time. Your interest in hedge funds has made this book possible, and I thank you very much for your pursuit of this fascinating subject.

Like it or not, hedge funds are here to stay. As an investment vehicle they are no longer considered an alternative investment but rather an important investment in a diversified portfolio. And although hedge funds have not yet become traditional, in the months and years ahead I believe that the differences that separate traditional investment funds or mutual funds and hedge funds are going to become smaller and smaller. Hedge funds, no matter what the people in Washington say or the popular press writes, are not going anywhere because people understand the value of creating a portfolio that is hedged against market volatility and provides an opportunity to make money regardless of which way the market is moving. Hedge funds are now being used by investors of all shapes and sizes and play an important role in the future of the financial markets around the globe.

To write this book I called on many of the usual suspects who have helped me over the years to make me look good in print. Without their help, I probably would not have been able to complete this project. They are of course Viki Goldman, the greatest librarian and researcher I have ever known and Sam Graff, the only true newspaper man I know in the tri-state area. Thank you both for the hard work you perform to make my work better. I truly appreciate it.

The people at Wiley have once again provided a platform for my work and to all of them, I say thank you. I hope the book is all you intended it to be when you gave me the go-ahead to write it.

I want to thank my family for their support and guidance over the years. It is through your efforts that this book, as well as the others, have been possible.

And finally to Felice, all I can say is thank you for being a provider of inspiration and support to see this project through. I appreciate your effort to keep Leah and Jonah out of the attic so I could complete the manuscript in time to hit the deadline, as well as your willingness to allow me to pursue my dreams day in and day out.

Daniel A. Strachman
Fanwood, NJ
October 2010

Introduction

Why Hedge Funds Now and Forever?

Over the past 10 years, hedge funds have gone from relative obscurity to being a topic of cocktail party chatter and the place to work on the Street to being blamed for everything that is wrong in the world of finance and beyond. Hardly a day goes by without a report of how hedge funds and those who provide services to them are reaping benefits on the backs of unsuspecting and unwilling victims around the globe. In the wake of the credit crisis and the government-led bailout of the banks, hedge funds and those who manage and invest in them have become the most talked about investment products since the Internet initial public offerings (IPOs) of the technology boom.

The rise from obscurity began with the astronomical returns that many hedge funds posted during the euphoria that swept the investment world at the close of the last century and the new century's first decade. These outsized returns have led to interest by investors of all shapes and sizes in years leading up to the credit crisis. In the post–credit crisis environment, interest in hedge funds and those who manage these—often thought of as secretive—investment vehicles has been sparked by the opposite: losses racked up in the past few years by many of the hedge fund world's most famous and sought-after managers. At the beginning of the new millennium, the issues for investors were "How do I invest?" and "How much can I expect?" At the halfway point of the decade the issues had become "How do I get my money out?" and "Is there anything left?" At the end of the decade, the issue was "What happened to the money?"

After the technology bubble burst and investors realized that there was more to making money in the markets than simply buying companies with .com in their names, they began to look to alternative investments as ways to juice the returns of their portfolios. In this case, the alternative investment happened to be anything and everything that was not considered a mutual fund or exchange traded fund.

Why did investors look to hedge funds for returns? The answer is the same as that given by Willie Sutton when he was asked why he robbed banks—because that's where the money is or is perceived to be on Wall Street.

Unlike the technology bubble that lasted a mere three years, the hedge fund craze is not a bubble, and people realized that these things are here to stay. Once again, the greed that was deemed good in the 1980s came back in favor among investors regardless of Washington's attempt to thwart it.

However, instead of hoping to ride the tails of takeover artists and leveraged buyout kings, today's investors are looking to hedge fund managers for the returns they so desperately crave.

Over the years, hedge fund managers, like most money managers as a group, have experienced their ups and downs. As I covered in previous editions of this book, at the end of the twentieth century and the early part of the twenty-first century many of the investment world's biggest and brightest hedge fund managers posted significant losses and in some cases were forced to liquidate their hedge funds. Many did not recover or, worse still, recovered only to be busted in the recent credit crisis and market meltdown.

Today as then, investors do not want to believe that these so-called Midas traders could make such drastic mistakes and run into so much trouble. Since the initial stories broke and the bailout was implemented, the markets have turned for the better. As can be expected, some funds were able to stop the hemorrhaging at the end of 2008 and experienced stellar returns in 2009.

Those fund managers who did not suffer massive losses in 2008 have seen their funds grow by leaps and bounds in terms of assets under management while those who got spanked by the market—well let's just say, these folks are looking for work these days.

In the midst of the carnage many pundits believed that the hedge fund business was finished. The truth is exactly the opposite. Hedge funds are here to stay. Sure, some may be wiped out or close their doors either voluntarily or because investors forced a liquidation of the portfolios, but there will always be someone willing to open another hedge fund and companies willing to work with the budding manager.

prime broker

a service offered by brokerage firms provide clearance, settlement, trading, and custody functions for hedge funds.

Not only are hedge funds thriving, but so are the service providers. Prime brokers, administrators, lawyers, and accountants as well as real estate agents, headhunters, marketers, and insurance people are all ready, willing, and able to provide for a hedge fund manager's every need.

The reason?

Wall Street is about making money—and running a hedge fund provides one of the greatest ways to do it, and providing services to those who run hedge funds is also quite lucrative.

This book is intended to provide an overview of the hedge fund industry. It covers many of the most important subjects surrounding running and investing in these investment vehicles. Certainly there is no one way to invest in hedge funds, as there are so many different funds with just as many different investment strategies and philosophies. A key goal of this book is to provide an objective view of the industry, one that gives you an understanding of the complex world of hedge funds that has dramatically changed since the concept was created in the late 1940s.

The growing importance and impact of hedge funds make it a subject that all investors should seek to understand. That's especially true in light of the credit crisis and because there are so many misconceptions about the industry.

Today, many people outside Wall Street believe that Bernie Madoff, Long-Term Capital Management LP, and George Soros are the sole representatives of the entire hedge fund industry. This is just not the case.

Although it is difficult to give an exact number, for the purposes of this book let's say that there are more than 8,000 hedge funds with more than a trillion dollars in assets under management. While firms like Soros, Paulson, Maverick, Tiger, and Tudor are generally considered to be the most famous hedge fund managers and most respected, people like Madoff, KL, and Bayou are probably the most notorious fraudsters to use the hedge fund moniker to perpetuate their dirty deeds. However, all of these are a far cry from representing the entire industry. The hedge fund industry stretches all over the world and ranges from men and women who manage titanic sums of money to those who manage a relative pittance.

Madoff in fact did not run a hedge fund but rather was a simple fraudster who managed money for a hedge fund of funds and separate accounts for his victims. Most people get his story wrong. The public believes that Madoff was a hedge fund manager and this belief has put a black eye on the industry. Madoff was a common thief on a grand scale who used the trappings of Wall Street to steal—that is it, nothing more or less. He just did it on a grander scale than anyone.

The common perception about the hedge fund industry is quite different from reality. The perception of the hedge fund industry is that of money managers who are gunslingers and buccaneers, secretly trading billions of dollars by the seat of their pants with little if any thought to risk because of the potential reward.

The reality is that most hedge funds have far less than $500 million in assets under management and, in most cases, every single trade that is executed is a calculated move—one in which risk and reward have been measured before a buy or sell order is placed. It seems that regardless of how often a hedge fund manager talks to the press or appears on one of the financial news networks, the industry cannot seem to shed the stigma of being made up of gunslingers and buccaneers who operate in a secret world.

A careful look at many hedge fund managers, however, will show that there is probably more risk to investing in an ordinary mutual fund than in most hedge funds because hedge funds are able to go both long and short the market. Mutual fund managers are generally only able to go one way—long the market, which means that should the market enter a prolonged period of negative returns it will be extremely difficult for the mutual fund manager to put up positive numbers—whereas a hedge fund manager can take advantage of the downside by going short.

Another critical difference between hedge funds and mutual funds is that in most cases, hedge fund managers put most if not all of their own capital or net worth into their own fund. In short, they put their money where their mouths are. The losses or gains directly affect the size of their own bank accounts along with those of their investors. The same cannot be said for most mutual funds and those who manage these types of products.

People who think that hedge funds are run by ruthless men and women looking to make a buck at any cost do not understand the basic concept of hedge fund management. Although a few managers may operate in this fashion, most do not. Most are interested in two things: preserving capital and making money for their partners. The hedge fund industry is a stay-rich business—not a get-rich business. If you ask managers what is the most important aspect of their business, they will tell you: the preservation of capital. It takes money to make money. If you lose capital, you limit your resources to invest further and you soon will be out of business.

By limiting risk and not betting the ranch on a single investment, they will live to invest another day. For hedge fund managers, slow and steady wins the race. The men and women who run hedge funds are some of the most dedicated money managers in the world. This dedication shows in their ability to continually outperform the market.

There is a big difference between hedge funds and mutual funds. The first is the size of the industry. The largest hedge fund complex has more than $80 billion in assets under management while the largest mutual fund complex has more than $2.7 trillion in assets under management.[1]

All mutual funds are highly regulated by the Securities and Exchange Commission (SEC) and are open to any and all investors, assuming they can meet the minimum investment requirements. Hedge funds are not open to the general public, only to accredited investors, super-accredited investors, and institutions.

There are a number of different types of accredited investors—both individuals and institutions. Individual accredited investors are defined by the SEC as a natural person with income of $200,000 (with a spouse $300,000) in the past two years and have reasonable expectations of continued income at that level and a net worth of $1,000,000.[2] Institutions are defined as being accredited investors if they fall into a number of different categories, including but not limited to the following definitions:[3] In Dodd-Frank Act—commonly referred to as the Financial Reform Act, that President Obama signed into law in July 2010—an investor can not include the value of his or her primary residence when determining if their net worth meets the requirement set forth in the law.

1. A bank, insurance company, registered investment company, business development company, or small business investment company.
2. A charitable organization, corporation, or partnership with assets of more than $5 million.
3. A business in which all the equity owners are accredited investors.

Hedge funds are not allowed to advertise—which is why you do not see billboards or television commercials for managers and their funds.

For the most part, the SEC does not allow mutual fund managers to use derivatives or to sell securities short to enhance performance. This is a major difference.

Hedge funds can use any legal means necessary to produce results. Most mutual fund managers are paid on the basis of the amount of assets they attract, while hedge fund managers are paid for performance.

Unlike mutual fund investing, hedge fund investing is about calculating how to perform in good and bad markets through the use of investment strategies that consist of *long positions* and *short positions.* Whereas mutual fund managers are limited to taking long positions in stocks and bonds, hedge fund managers are able to use a much more extensive array of investment strategies such as the use of shorting and derivatives. It is all about capital preservation and healthy returns.

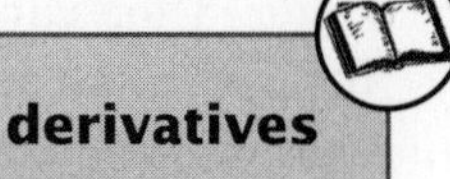

derivatives
securities that take their values from another security.

In the large hedge fund complexes, accountability for the funds rests with multiple managers, analysts, and traders. In smaller organizations, a single individual is accountable for the funds. Most hedge fund organizations usually consist of a small staff working with the manager. While the size and scope of the organizations vary, all hedge funds seek to provide investors with a valuable service: capital preservation mixed with healthy returns. The common theme among all hedge fund managers is to use investment strategies that create a diversified portfolio that over time will outperform the market regardless of market conditions.

long position
a transaction to purchase shares of a stock resulting in a net positive position.

short position

a transaction to sell shares of stock that the investor does not own.

The purpose of this book is to provide an introduction that explores these types of operations. I purposely did not examine managers and funds that are covered in the popular press. Instead I spent time getting to know managers who are known on Wall Street but not outside it. They manage portfolios ranging in size from $2 million to over $2 billion. In some cases they operate by themselves out of a small office with one assistant. Others have multiple offices around the globe with staffs of a hundred or more.

The idea of the book is to provide you with a clearer view of how these people operate in the various markets that they trade. Because each employs different trading methodologies and investment philosophies, this book provides you with a unique look at the business of managing money. It will, I hope, give you the insight you need to find alternative means to achieve your investment goals. While all the managers are different, they all have two things in common: They use some piece of the same business model, and each is an entrepreneur.

While profiles of managers make up a significant portion of this book, other pages describe the history of the industry and how it has evolved. George Soros, Michael Steinhardt, and Julian Robertson, unlike what many have been led to believe, did not create the hedge fund industry. They may have advanced the concept, but the idea and the term were created by journalist Alfred Winslow Jones, a visionary who used his knowledge of sociology and his reporting skills to come up with the idea in the late 1940s while researching an article for Fortune magazine.

Jones's basic concept was simple: By combining the use of long and short positions coupled with the use of leverage, a manager should be able to outperform the market in good times and to limit losses in bad times. Today most hedge funds employ the same concept. Like everything else, however, each manager uses his or her own unique style; and therefore some may use more leverage than others, and some may not go short at all. All are out to beat the indexes while limiting losses. The right way to look at hedge fund performance is by absolute returns, regardless of market conditions.

leverage

a means of enhancing return or value without increasing investment. Buying securities on margin is an example of leverage.

Hedge funds continue to thrive because this concept works.

Evidence lies in the number of people and firms that have grown to support hedge funds. Many of these supporting cast members believe that providing goods and services to the industry will be just as profitable as investing in or operating a hedge fund. These people range from consultants and brokers to lawyers and accountants. It is very easy to find a firm that will not only recommend a manager to potential investors but also help a manager find office space, set up phone lines, and install computers. People from all walks of Wall Street have gotten into the hedge fund business, making it relatively easy not only to open a hedge fund but to learn about and invest in one as well.

To understand how hedge funds operate, you need to understand the styles and strategies their managers use. While most conventional money managers own securities in hopes of price appreciation, many hedge fund managers employ alternative strategies that do not rely on the market going up: short selling, risk arbitrage, and the trading of derivatives. Most hedge funds employ strategies that allow them to hedge against risk to ensure that no matter which way the market moves, they are protected against loss.

arbitrage

a financial transaction involving simultaneous purchase in one market and sale in a different market.

There are many benefits to investing in hedge funds.

I believe, and am not alone mind you, that the best and brightest minds in money management have migrated from around Wall Street to the hedge fund industry. Paying managers for performance ensures that the investor is going to get the fairest shake and that their interest is aligned with the investor's. Add the fact that managers have their own money in the fund and that they can go long and short, which allows them to profit from the up and downside of the market, and that should be enough for investors to know that their money is in good hands. However, due diligence is still required before each and every investment, and only once it passes your test is it worthy of your money.

As an investor, you need to understand what you are getting into and be willing to do research to learn about the manager and the various strategies employed. One of the biggest mistakes people make with any kind of investment is not taking the time to do research. A smart investor is a well-researched investor. If a manager is unwilling to spend time discussing strategy, skills, and background, then investors probably should look elsewhere.

Another mistake is chasing so-called hot money—which is money that flows to the best-performing manager for a quarter or two. The right thing to do is to find managers who perform consistently over time. As an investor you should expect up months and quarters and down months and quarters and, more important, information regarding both periods. It is important to understand where the manager's performance is or is not coming from.

One of the basic tenets of sound investing is portfolio diversification. You should expect managers to explain how they employ it in their portfolios.

One of the greatest lessons of the near self-destruction of Long-Term Capital Management LP is the need for investors to understand how and where their money is being invested. Madoff, while not a hedge fund, mastered this as well, although he did the opposite: Instead of telling his investors that they were too stupid to understand what was happening with the money, he buried them in paper.

In either case the idea that a manager wants an investor to have blind faith is ridiculous. Managers should be held accountable, and investors should demand to know what is being done with their money.

Despite lapses by some managers and all the negative media attention, not to mention the attacks by Congress and a number of State Attorneys General, writing the third edition of this book has made it even more obvious to me that hedge funds are good for investors and managers alike. I believe that by the time you are done reading this book you will believe this as well. Throughout the text you may have questions about hedge funds, the economy, or politics. If you do, please feel free to email me at: das@hedgeanswers.com.

Chapter 1

Hedge Fund Basics

It seems to me that the only time the press mentions hedge funds is when one blows up or some sort of crisis hits one of the world's many markets or there is a fraud and investors are robbed or taken to the cleaners. This has been a constant by the media since the summer of 1998.

Step back if you will to the summer of 1998, when Charlton Heston took over the presidency of the National Rifle Association, Compaq Computer bought Digital Equipment Corporation for nine billion dollars, the largest deal in the industry at the time, and the United States embassies in Tanzania and Kenya were bombed, killing 224 people and injuring over 4,500. It was also during this time that a currency crisis in Asia spread to Russia, then crept into Europe, and finally hit the shores of the United States in mid-July and early August.

Many who follow the markets assumed that things were bad and were going to stay that way for a very long time. And of course the first people who were looked at when the volatility hit and markets dropped were members of the hedge fund community. Although no one knew for sure what was going on and who and how much was lost, one thing was clear: Many of the most famous hedge funds of the time were in serious trouble.

After weeks of speculation and rumors, the market finally heard the truth: The world's "greatest investor" and his colleagues had made a mistake of significant proportions.

At a little before 4 P.M. Eastern Standard Time (EST) on Wednesday, August 26, 1992, Stanley Druckenmiller made the announcement on CNBC in a matter-of-fact way: The Soros organization, in particular its flagship hedge fund, the Quantum Fund, had lost more than $2 billion in recent weeks in the wake of the currency crisis in Russia. The fund had invested heavily in the Russian markets and the trades had gone against them. When the ruble collapsed, the liquidity dried up, and there was nothing left to do but hold on to a bunch of worthless slips of paper. During the interview, Druckenmiller did mention that although the fund had sustained significant losses in its Russian investments, overall its total return was still positive for the year, with gains upwards of 19 percent. However, in the months that followed, the Soros organization announced significant changes to the operation, including closing one fund that lost over 30 percent.

When asked by the CNBC reporter where the losses came from, Druckenmiller was not specific. It appeared that it was not one trade but a series of trades that had gone against them. The next day, the *New York Times* reported that the fund had also posted losses in dollar bond trades.

When Druckenmiller made the announcement, the Russian equity markets had been down over 80 percent and the government had frozen currency trading as well as stopped paying interest on its debts. The Asian flu had spread, and Russia and many of the other former Soviet republics looked to be in trouble. The difference was that in Russia and the surrounding countries, things looked quite a bit worse than in east Asia.

Although there had been rumors of hedge fund misfortunes and mistakes in these regions, no one knew the true size and scope of the losses. Druckenmiller's announcement was the tip of a very big iceberg and the beginning of a trend in the hedge fund industry, one that was a first: to be open and honest about losses. Hedge fund managers en masse seemed to be stepping up to the plate and admitting publicly that they had made mistakes and had sustained significant losses.

The day after the Soros organization spoke up, a number of other hedge fund managers issued similar statements. Druckenmiller's interview turned out to be the first of several such admissions of losses by famed fund managers. And the losses were staggering.

One fund lost over 85 percent of its assets, going from over $300 million under management to around $25 million. Another said it had lost over $200 million. Others lost between 10 and 20 percent of their assets. They all had come out publicly to lick their wounds, a sort of Wall Street mea culpa.

When the carnage first hit, it seemed that everyone except Julian Robertson, the mastermind behind Tiger Management, the largest hedge fund complex in the world at the time, was the only "name" fund manager not to post losses. Yet even that proved not to be true.

In a statement on September 16, 1998, Robertson said that his funds had lost $2.1 billion or 10 percent of the $20-odd billion he had under management. The losses seemed to come in the early part of September and stemmed from a long-profitable bet on the yen's continuing to fall against the dollar. Because the yen instead appreciated, a number of Robertson's trades declined in value.[1] The funds also saw losses on trades executed in Hong Kong when government authorities intervened in the stock and futures markets to ward off foreign speculators.

Still, like Soros, Tiger was up significantly for the first eight months of 1998. These numbers echoed the funds' performance in recent years with returns in 1996 of over 38 percent and in 1997 of 56 percent. In a letter to investors explaining the losses, Robertson cautioned that the volatility of various markets would make it difficult to continue to post positive returns month after month.

"Sometimes we are going to have a very bad month," he wrote. "We are going to lose money in Russia and in our U.S. longs, and the diversification elsewhere is not going to make up for that, at least not right away. You should be prepared for this."

One of Robertson's investors, who requested anonymity, said that she could not believe all the bad press Robertson received for admitting to the losses. She also questioned whether the reporters really knew what they were talking about when they wrote stories on hedge funds.

"He had some losses, but he is also having a very good year," she said. "The press treats him unfairly because they don't understand what he does or how he does it. They also don't understand how he could be up so much when the mutual funds they themselves are investing in are not performing as well."

However, things were worse at Tiger than the public believed. On November 2, 1998, *The Wall Street Journal* ran a story titled "Robertson's Funds Become Paper Tigers as Blue October Leads to Red Ink for '98." According to the story, the funds had lost over 17 percent, or about $3.4 billion through October, which wiped out all of the funds' gains for the year. The funds' total losses through the end of October were approximately $5.5 billion, leaving Tiger with assets of around $17 billion, and it was expected to post losses of 3 percent for the month of November. By the middle of December the funds were down approximately 4 percent for the year.[2] On top of the losses, the funds also faced a number of withdrawals from investors both in the United States and abroad. Although a number of industry watchers and observers seemed to believe that Tiger had significant amounts of withdrawals, the firm's public relations firm denied that this was the case. The spokesperson did say that the funds did have "some withdrawals but nothing significant."

Robertson's letter to investors seemed to be the only words of wisdom that investors, traders, and brokers could hold on to as the carnage in the hedge fund industry unfolded. Every day for the next four or five weeks, the financial pages were filled with stories similar to the tales of Robertson's and Soros' woes.

After all the dust settled and the losses were realized, the hedge fund industry entered its dark period, a direct result of the losses that many big funds posted and the fact that it was the dawn of the technology stock where no investor could do wrong. This period lasted until the tech bubble burst and investors realized that they needed professionals handling their money and that they could not make money on their own. However, in spite of the years that followed the collapse of Russia, it was clear that Soros and Robertson, both true money masters, and others like them were going to give way to a new breed of managers. The stimulus for this change in the industry was the result of the following incident. The next 10 years saw a series of ups and downs for the hedge fund industry—mostly ups. The industry and those who relied on hedge funds continued to thrive well into the 21st century. However, as the first decade of the new millennium drew to a close, the hedge fund industry and much of the financial systems were turned upside down.

In some ways one could say the events of the summer of 1998 prepared the powers that be and investors around the globe for the events that occurred during the credit crisis of 2008 and the revelation of the Madoff fraud. In order to understand why, one needs to first look at an event that shocked the world 10 years earlier.

The Near Collapse of Long-Term Capital Management

For most of the summer of 1998, the news about the financial markets was not good. Although many expected to see a recovery in the third and fourth quarter, things took a turn for the worse on September 21, 1998, when the story broke that a large hedge fund was about to collapse and take markets around the globe with it.

For weeks leading up to that Monday, there had been speculation that Long-Term Capital Management LP (LTCM), a hedge fund with more than $3 billion in assets and run by one of Wall Street's smartest traders, was on the brink of collapse. Earlier in the summer, the firm had announced that it had lost over 44 percent of its assets. Rumors about it not being able to meet *margin calls* were running rampant through Wall Street.

The first real signs that something was dreadfully wrong came when the press broke a story that the New York Stock Exchange had launched an inquiry to determine if the fund was meeting its margin calls from brokers. There had been speculation that some of the brokers were giving Long-Term Capital special treatment and not making it meet its margin obligations, and the NYSE was trying to find out if it was true.

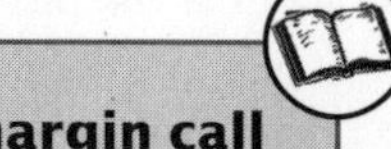

margin call

demand that an investor deposit enough money or securities to bring a margin account up to the minimum maintenance requirements.

Initially, things at the fund seemed to be under control. It was believed that its managers had put a stop to the hemorrhaging and its operation was returning to normal. These rumors were part truth and part myth. Nobody on Wall Street—not the traders, not the brokers, and least of all the firms that had lent to Long-Term Capital—wanted to believe that it was in dire straits. This was not some whiz kid trader who had just gotten out of business school and was flying by the seat of his pants. This was John Meriwether, the person who had invented and mastered the use of rocket science to make significant returns while limiting risk.

The fund was more than Meriwether; it was managed by some of the smartest minds around Wall Street's trading desks. At the time, Long-Term Capital's partners list read like a who's who of Wall Street's elite. People like Robert Merton and Myron Scholes, both Nobel economics laureates, as well as David Mullins, a former vice chairman of the Federal Reserve Board, were the people making trading decisions and managing its assets. And there were a number of former Salomon Brothers trading whizzes as well as a handful of Ph.D.s whom Meriwether had groomed personally.

How could this fund blow up? The question seemed ludicrous, especially because the market conditions that existed had often proved to be the ones in which this kind of fund thrived. Wall Street believed that it was impossible for Meriwether to be going the way of Victor Niederhoffer or David Askin—two other high-profile hedge fund managers who lost everything when funds they operated blew up in the mid-1990s.

Everyone, including himself, believed that Meriwether was the king of quants, as traders who use *quantitative analysis* and mathematics are called, a true master of the universe. People believed that the press had gotten things wrong and that of course the fund would be able to weather the storm.

quantitative analysis

security analysis that uses objective statistical information to determine when to buy and sell securities.

"He has done it before," they said. "Of course he will do it again." Yet by the end of September 1998, there was one word to describe the previous statement: *wrong.*

The markets had gotten the best of Meriwether and his partners. He and his team of Ph.D.s and Nobel laureates had made mistakes that could not be reversed. They had bet the farm and then some and were on the brink of losing it all. The problem was a combination of leverage, risk, and, of course, greed—three ingredients that when mixed together produce one thing: unsustainable losses.

The first news stories came out in late August and early September, after Meriwether announced in a letter to investors that the fund had lost a significant amount of assets. In his letter, which was subsequently published on Bloomberg, Meriwether blamed a number of circumstances for the losses. Still, he said, he and his colleagues and partners believed that the markets would turn in their favor; as long as they continued on the same path, investors would see light at the end of a very dark tunnel.

The letter stated, "Losses of this magnitude are a shock to us as they surely are to you," and that although the firm prided itself on its ability to post returns that are not correlated to the global bond, stock, or currency markets, too much happened too quickly for it to make things right. As with most of Meriwether's communications with investors, the letter did not delve into the types of trades or markets in which the fund was investing. The letter also did not discuss the amounts of leverage Long-Term Capital was using in its drive to capture enormous profits with even the slightest uptick. Nor did it explain that Meriwether had started to trade stock arbitrage positions, something completely different from the bond and currency plays with which he earned his stripes. The letter also failed to mention that the fund had borrowed money from itself to cover its operating expenses.

The simplest explanation of what happened to LTCM is that because multiple markets were hit with multiple crises at the same time—a perfect storm, if you will—there was no way for it to limit its losses or make money. Everything LTCM tried to do failed. Basically, everything that could have gone wrong did. Although the firm specialized in finding unique situations regardless of the condition of the market and employed many "if, then" scenarios, the one thing the partners never were able to figure out was what to do if everything they planned for happened at the same time. The strength of Long-Term Capital's operation rested on the managers' ability to determine what would happen to the prices of many securities when various events hit the market, but their black boxes never told them what would occur if everything they thought possible happened at the same time.

For example, it was widely reported that the fund was short U.S. Treasuries and long high-yield paper and other more risky illiquid investments. The idea was that as Treasury prices fell, yields would increase and the other types of debt instruments would rise in price.

The exact opposite happened. When the turmoil hit the markets, there was an immediate flight to quality, resulting in a significant increase in Treasury prices and a significant decrease in prices of riskier investments. Instead of converging, the trade diverged and ended up going in the wrong direction on both sides of the ticket. When prices of Treasuries shoot up, the yield goes down, and likewise when the prices of high-yield debt go down, the yield increases. Markets that were illiquid to begin with became even more illiquid, and the Treasury market, which has enormous liquidity at all times, showed its lowest yields in a generation.

To understand how the firm could have lost so much so quickly and supposedly even put the world markets at great risk, one first needs to understand how Long-Term Capital operated. The firm specialized in bond arbitrage, a trading strategy Meriwether mastered while working at Salomon Brothers in the 1980s. Traders, using very complex mathematical formulas, capitalize on small price discrepancies among securities in various markets. The idea is to exploit the prices of certain bonds by buying or selling the security based on the perceived value, not the current market value.

The idea behind Long-Term Capital from its outset was to employ this strategy to capture significant profits while enjoying insignificant amounts of risk. Meriwether and his partners were not interested in making a killing on a single trade but rather in picking up small amounts with relatively minor swings in the market from multiple trades. The idea was to employ enough leverage that even the slightest market movement would cause the firm to profit quite handsomely.

If they bought a stock at $100, they would not wait for it to go to $120 or $180 but rather would sell out when it hit $101. Making a dollar does not seem like much, but because their leverage was in excess of 20 to 1 they were able to make big profits on the very small (1 percent) movement. With $100 of equity, the fund would have been able to control $2,000 worth of stock. So in this hypothetical situation, the profit would have been approximately 20 percent. If a $100 investment leveraged at 20 to 1 goes up 10 percent, the trade yields a $200 profit, or a yield of 200 percent on the initial $100, a tripling in value.[3]

In the aftermath of the fund's meltdown, there was of course a lot of Monday morning quarterbacking with very little explanation of what went wrong. The *New York Times* managed to get some unique color on the situation:

> As one Salomon Brothers veteran described it, [Meriwether's] fund was like a roulette player betting on red and doubling up its bets each time the wheel stopped on black. "A gambler with $1,000 will probably lose," he said. "A gambler with $1 billion will wind up owning the casino, because it is a mathematical certainty that red will come up eventually—but you have to have enough chips to stay at the table until that happens."[4]

One thing for sure is that to stay at the table, Meriwether used significant amounts of leverage. The problem was that at Long-Term Capital, leverage got out of hand.

The first indication that things had taken a turn for the worse was in July 1998. Meriwether announced that the fund had posted a loss of some $300 million for the month of June. It was the first time the fund had posted a loss for a month since its inception four years earlier. Reports at the time questioned the veil of secrecy that surrounded the fund's trading and it was unclear where the losses were coming from. The fund had operated in complete silence when it came to discussing strategy or positions, because it believed that once people understood where it was making money, they could determine where its next moves would be and copy its strategies. Very few outside Meriwether's inner circle knew what markets the fund was trading in and where profits and losses originated.

Initial reports had the losses coming from the turmoil that rocked the mortgage-backed securities markets. Still, because of the size of the losses, people suspected that the firm had losses elsewhere, including the currency and U.S. Treasuries markets.

It was quite a shock to many on Wall Street when the losses were announced. For years, Long-Term Capital had performed extremely well and its leader was considered to be too smart to make mistakes. Many others could make mistakes and fail but not John Meriwether and his quants. Wall Street believed that these men and women walked on water. The firm perpetuated the myth time and time again by putting up strong returns, no matter what the condition of the market.

In 1995, the firm was up over 42 percent, net of fees, while in 1996 and 1997 it was up 41 percent and 17 percent respectively. Long-Term Capital did not just beat the indexes; it trounced them.

Still, never would the statement "Past performance is no indication of future results" become more pertinent than during the summer of 1998.

On a very hot day in August, a person I was interviewing for the first edition of this book told me that Long-Term Capital's losses for June were just the tip of the iceberg; the firm had sustained enormous losses the previous Friday when buyers dumped corporate bonds and bought Treasuries, sending yields to their lowest point in 20 years. The person told me that a friend had just come from a meeting with a New York investor who said he was pulling out of Long-Term Capital and that Meriwether was on the verge of bankruptcy. I was shocked. On my way out of the interview, I immediately called friends at New York newspapers to try the story. It was possible that other superstars had blown up and of course many smaller hedge funds run by inexperienced managers had failed.

The thought of LTCM failing was ridiculous—it just did not make sense. Its managers were some of the best and brightest on the Street, and it just did not seem possible. However, by mid-morning the story had been confirmed; a number of people said that the fund had posted significant losses and looked to be going under.

The next day a number of stories appeared in the papers confirming that Meriwether had lost a significant amount and that the fund needed a large capital infusion to stay afloat. Things looked quite grim for the fund.

It was the first indication that September was going to be a very long month for Long-Term Capital's management and investors, its trading partners, and the entire hedge fund industry.

The story came out because someone leaked a letter that Meriwether had written to investors explaining the situation and requesting new capital. He asked that investors be patient and that they supply him with new capital to "take full advantage of this unusually attractive environment."

People who spoke with him about the letter explained that he believed that by attracting new capital, he would be able to put a hold on the losses and be able to take advantage of the inevitable turnaround that was about to come. However, others believed that it had the makings of a Ponzi scheme.

"By continuing to employ strategies that had worked in the past, John believed he would be able to recover from this dreadful situation," a hedge fund manager who is close to Meriwether said. "The problem was people had lost faith. Never had the statement 'you're only as good as your last trade' been more prevalent on Wall Street."

Acknowledgment of the problem came a little too late to stop the hemorrhaging. By the time Meriwether asked for more money, the losses were too great. Even if investors had decided to pony up the extra dollars, they would have only been able to stave off the inevitable for a little while because the need for cash was so great. The well had dried up and the opportunities, it seemed, no longer existed.

At the time he wrote to investors, Meriwether probably did not have any idea where the money to bail out his firm would come from nor the extent of what the bailout would cost. Besides looking for capital from his investors, Meriwether approached outsiders, including Warren Buffett and George Soros, all of whom turned him down.

Buffett did resurface, but as a potential purchaser of the operation, not as an investor. He, along with Goldman Sachs Group LP and American International Group Inc., offered to buy the entire operation from Meriwether and to assume the fund's massive portfolios. Meriwether said no, because he did not want to give up control. The press seemed to believe that Meriwether's ego had gotten in the way of getting the deal done with Buffett.

The situation came to a head on Monday, September 21, 1998, when Wall Street's most powerful and influential players got calls from representatives of the Federal Reserve Bank of New York. Some of the recipients were surprised that the Fed was going to intervene in a situation over which it had no direct control.

The president of the New York Fed requested that Wall Street's elite meet to discuss the fate of one of its own. Not since the days of J. P. Morgan had such a group of Wall Street moguls assembled in one room with the intention of devising a plan to save an institution as well as possibly themselves.

Initially, people credited the New York Fed as the stimulus for the bailout, but subsequent reports credited John Corzine, co-managing partner at Goldman Sachs and future senator from New Jersey, as the person who got the ball rolling. Still, it is believed that the Fed prompted him after it started questioning the amount of money Long-Term Capital owed companies under its supervision. It has been suggested that both Goldman Sachs and Merrill Lynch & Co. Inc. had been on the brink of losing so much money because of Long-Term Capital's inability to pay that the Federal Reserve was worried that the firms might themselves be pushed to the brink of insolvency should the fund go bankrupt. Unlike other bankruptcies, when hedge funds go out of business all of their positions are liquidated immediately, in most cases at fire-sale prices. It is unknown exactly how much money was at stake, but it is clear that trillions of dollars would have been wiped out if there had been a forced liquidation.

It was also clear that the fund had come to the end of its rope. It needed money to meet its margin obligations or else havoc would reign over the world's already tumultuous markets. For the first time in a very long time the federal government determined that an organization was "too big to fail," and it was going to do everything in its power to ensure that it did not fail. Prior to its involvement in the LTCM bailout, the federal government had deemed Chrysler too big to fail and bailed the struggling car maker out in the 1970s with a series of loan guarantees and contracts.

Did the Fed do the right thing? The people I spoke with seemed divided on the issue. Although the debate will go on for some time, one thing is for sure: In light of the takeover by the consortium, Long-Term Capital was able to right itself and started earning money again in the fourth quarter of 1998.

The Federal Reserve had hoped that Goldman Sachs would find a buyer for the fund, but when that failed, it asked the dozen or so companies to come up with a workable solution to this very serious problem.

When the announcement was made that the potential buyer had walked, David Komansky, chairman of Merrill Lynch at the time, took over the discussion to determine to what extent the companies would contribute to keep Long-Term Capital alive and possibly keep a number of themselves from collapsing as well.

After much discussion, including some who said they did not want to participate in the bailout but had their minds changed, 14 companies decided to contribute to the bailout, committing sums ranging from \$100 million to \$350 million. One that did not participate was Bear Stearns & Co., Inc. It

TABLE 1.1 Bailout of Long-Term Capital Management

$100 Million	$300 Million
Bangque Paribas	Bankers Trust
Crédit Agricole	Barclays
Lehman Brothers	Chase Manhattan
	Credit Suisse First Boston
$125 Million	Deutsche Bank
Société Générale	Goldman Sachs
	JPMorgan
	Merrill Lynch
	Morgan Stanley
	Salomon Smith Barney
	Union Bank of Switzerland

Source: Wall Street Journal, November 16, 1998.

was agreed that it should not chip in to the bailout because its risk as Long-Term Capital's clearing broker significantly outweighed the risk posed to other contributors. Table 1.1 illustrates to what extent each company contributed to the bailout.

Although—because of the secrecy surrounding the operation—it is unclear who lost what, it is apparent that many of Wall Street's most senior executives took some very big hits when the firm went down. The rescue plan reduced all of the investors' stakes to under 10 percent of what they had been. Executives of some of Wall Street's most prestigious companies—including Merrill Lynch, Bear Stearns, and PaineWebber Group Inc.—faced personal losses. A number of partners at the famed consulting firm McKinsey & Co. lost money as well.

The irony of the situation is that in the wake of the collapse, *The Wall Street Journal*, the *New York Times*, and the *New York Post* all reported that a number of investors were quite happy that earlier in 1998 Long-Term Capital had returned money to them. Yet most investors who received money back were quite upset at the time. In December 1997, Long-Term Capital had returned approximately $2.7 billion to investors ranging from small money managers to PaineWebber and the Bank of China.

The only firm on Wall Street that seemed to have done well with Long-Term Capital was PaineWebber.[5] It and its chairman and chief executive, Donald Marron, had invested $100 million and $10 million in the fund respectively. Both, however, received money back in 1997. According to a number of reports, the firm more than doubled its investment and Marron got enough money back to at least break even.

Other Wall Streeters were not so lucky. Bear Stearns chief executive James Cayne and executive vice president Warren Spector are believed to have lost more than $9 million each. Merrill Lynch's Komansky, who along with over a hundred of his colleagues had invested approximately $22 million in the fund, saw that position reduced to less than $2 million once the bailout was complete.

The idea that a hedge fund got too big to fail is quite remarkable. By the time the bailout agreement was reached, Long-Term Capital had received commitments in excess of $3.5 billion to be used to meet margin calls and to cover operating expenses. The bailout was designed to ensure that the firm would not collapse and cause credit markets around the world to cave in from dumping its positions. It is believed that if the fund had been forced to liquidate, it might have caused the undermining of more than $1 trillion in assets. However, this is pure speculation and we will never really know what could have happened had the fund truly gone down.

This experience makes it quite clear that the bull market of the mid- and late 1990s had gotten out of control and once again an enormous level of greed had come over the Street. The only way Long-Term Capital was able to become so large was that it was lent money without any regard for whether it could pay back what it borrowed. The lenders looked instead to the fees associated with the transactions and the continuous stream of revenue the firm would provide to line the brokerages' and banks' pockets.

In the wake of the Long-Term Capital disaster, the calls for hedge fund reform and regulation swept the nation and the world. Congress held hearings and industry observers cried foul, but hedge funds took a backseat to the scandal and impeachment that rocked the White House. Nothing came of the hearings and no new regulations were put in place.

The *New York Times* reported that one Wall Street executive who was briefed on the negotiations that led to the bailout said he had learned a lesson about his own firm's operation after reviewing its exposure to Long-Term Capital.

"We will never let our exposure to one counterparty get to these levels again—never. He had gotten too big for the market," he said of Meriwether. "Everybody gave him too much money."[6]

A few months after the bailout, however, things had started to turn around for Long-Term Capital Management and Meriwether. First the hedge fund reported profits and then came the speculation the fund was looking to buy out its saviors and that if an amicable arrangement could not be met, Meriwether would start a new investment vehicle. While the buyout never seemed to materialize, the fund's financial situation had completely turned around by the spring of 1999. Meriwether and his partners had paid back a significant portion of the bailout and had started talking about a new fund that they planned on launching.

In the early fall, Long-Term Capital had paid back close to 75 percent of the bailout to the consortium of financial institutions that had saved it a year earlier. The consortium issued a statement at the end of September stating that "the portfolio is in excellent shape" and that the risk profile of the fund had been reduced by nearly 90 percent. One of the stipulations of the bailout was that before Long-Term Capital's managers could operate a new fund, they had to repay 90 percent of the money the banks put into it. This meant that the fund needed to repay an additional $600 million to the consortium before Meriwether and his partners could raise money for a new fund.

By December 1999, LTCM fully repaid the banks that had prevented its collapse. Weeks later, the fund was quietly closed. Some investors are still sitting on losses. Meriwether has since gone on to launch a new hedge fund that employs similar investment strategies as LTCM called JWM Partners LLC.

The near collapse of LTCM set the stage for the future explosion of hedge fund managers and demand of investors for these sorts of investments.

Many market followers, historians, and practitioners like to say that the marker moves in cycles. Some say seven-year cycles, others say 10-year cycles. I am not sure—I am not a student of the markets—and therefore have no comment or view. I will say, however, people only seem to know that a cycle has ended after something has happened.

That being said, the bailout of LTCM created a precedent for the events of 2007 and 2008 to take place. In fact, some would say that bailing out a single hedge fund in 1998 provided the blue print for the bailout of the banks, auto makers, and mortgage lenders in 2008.

The Credit Crisis and Hedge Funds

One would have to have been hiding under a rock for the last 18 to 24 months to not have some view, idea, concept, or belief of what went wrong in the world to cause the collapse of Wall Street firms, the automakers, the mortgage industry, and the erosion of millions of jobs not just in the United States but around the world.

The world literally was turned upside down during this time and at the time of this writing, mid-2010 has still not recovered from the destruction, implosion, and nationalization of the financial industry.

Left was right, right was left, up was down, down was up, you get the drift. It was shocking, sad, and frustrating to watch the events unfold and witness the carnage literally right before all of our eyes.

The hedge fund industry took a lot and continues to receive quite a bit of flak for its role in the crisis and the potential for future problems due to leverage and lack of regulation. For awhile, Wall Street as a whole got the blame, however, in light of the political losses experienced by the Obama administration in early 2010, that tune had changed as well.

Hedge funds, Wall Street, and "greedy" bankers were still the cause of the problem according to most in Washington but now also the lack of regulation and the ability to enforce regulation is a big reason for the failures and erosion of capital.

It is all politics. Light a fire on the right so we don't see what is happening on the left. Regulation in particular is one subject that will be covered later in the book, but for now, remember this: Regulation is only as good as those who enforce it. If there is no enforcement, well, the regulation is worth little more than the paper it is written on.

The failure of two Bear Stearns hedge funds, the subsequent fire sale of the company to J.P. Morgan Chase, the bankruptcy of Lehman Brothers, and the bailout of many of the nations'—if not the worlds'—financial companies and automakers shocked most, if not all people, regardless of their economic strata or educational background.

Not since the Great Depression or at least in my lifetime, has there been such a level of government intervention into so many different areas of commerce. However, shocked as I was with "nationalization" of the banks by the Federal Government in the early part of the fall of 2008, what was more mind boggling and shocking was the failure of many hedge funds during this time. I am not talking about Madoff and the feeder funds here—this was a crime or at least fraud. I am talking about the inability of many of whom I believed were the best and brightest money managers in the world to make money during the volatility, and in turn post massive losses because of the failure.

Legends were smoked. Losses in the double digits were everywhere, and I for one was disgusted by this news as it flashed almost daily on my screens. I remember pulling into my garage in December 2008, and talking to a friend of mine who manages an endowment about the losses some of these "Hedge Fund Legends" had posted.

It was as if I just found out the Red Sox really did not win the World Series in 2004 and 2007. You see, unlike most people who follow sports and discuss game statistics with their friends, I follow managers. I discuss performance, strategy, and assets under management the way most people talk about hits, steals, and strikeouts. And just like people were devastated to learn of the fixing of the World Series by the Chicago White Sox in 1919, I was devastated when I heard and received reports about how bad these so-called hedge fund experts performed during 2007 and 2008.

The reality was that many of these so-called Legends and Brightest Managers turned out to be nothing more than closet indexers who run expensive mutual funds. They had sold me and their investors a bill of goods. This was never more apparent than when year-end numbers came out in early 2009.

According to The Barclay Hedge Fund Index, an index that measures the average performance of all hedge funds that report information to the company, the industry was down more than 21.63 percent.[7]

The hedge fund industry failed to deliver on its ability to make money in good and bad markets. The crisis caused many hedge funds to put up numbers that were just atrocious. The numbers at some of the most famous and respected hedge funds came in at year-end 2008 down 20 percent, down 30 percent, and, in one or two cases, down more than 50 percent. It was a bloodbath for investors and managers alike.

It frankly made me sick; I for one had always told people that one of the main reasons for investing in these sorts of investment vehicles was that when the market zigged, these investment vehicles zagged and vice versa. Well, in light of the numbers put up in 2008, that was just not the case.

I am not going to name names or provide details other than to say that many of the hedge funds that got clobbered in 2008 should have lost the faith of their investors. Much has been written about the losses experienced by many funds, funds that were not fraud per se—funds that simply did not know how to deal with volatility and as such seemed to be the last ones out of positions. The losses experienced by some of these funds are completely unacceptable, and investors need to take this abysmal performance into consideration prior to investing in any fund regardless of how they have recovered in 2009, 2010 and beyond.

There were some bright spots in the industry during the credit crisis, the most famous being John Paulson. His ability to call the credit crisis and stick with his call when people thought he was crazy and the positions moved against him is something completely unique. Paulson showed his investors that he had conviction and was willing to stick with his research and hypothesis regardless of what the rest of the Street was saying. I applaud him for his efforts. He is a rare find in today's crowded marketplace of managers. However, that being said, remember past performance is not an indication of future performance. Lightning does not often strike the same place twice, and therefore due diligence still needs to be completed. One of the best lessons to come out of the devastation and fraud was the need for thorough and continued due diligence.

One needs to understand what is happening with the money and get answers to the questions about strategy creation and implementation.

The credit crisis as a whole and its effect on hedge funds has been covered ad nauseum by most of the major media outlets, the popular press, the not-so-popular press, and in books, magazine articles, and blogs.

My belief is that once the credit crisis hit and we saw just how bad some of these managers performed, we all received a wake-up call for better due diligence. Never before has it been more important to perform due diligence and get under the skin of the managers and how they manage money. Due

TABLE 1.2 Barclay Hedge Fund Index Historical Data

	Jan	*Feb*	*Mar*	*Apr*	*May*	*Jun*	*Jul*	*Aug*	*Sep*	*Oct*	*Nov*	*Dec*
1997	3.620%	1.180%	–0.990%	0.490%	4.060%	3.110%	4.700%	0.520%	4.050%	–1.270%	–0.190%	1.290%
1998	–0.190%	3.760%	3.540%	1.150%	–1.680%	0.230%	–0.460%	–7.810%	1.050%	2.170%	3.780%	2.950%
1999	2.230%	–0.840%	3.480%	4.920%	1.150%	4.130%	0.820%	0.320%	0.740%	1.900%	5.330%	7.730%
2000	0.950%	6.760%	1.740%	–1.470%	–1.000%	3.260%	0.060%	3.740%	–0.710%	–1.070%	–2.520%	2.200%
2001	3.040%	–1.440%	–1.110%	2.020%	1.470%	0.510%	–0.570%	–0.180%	–2.580%	1.840%	2.020%	1.710%
2002	0.660%	–0.480%	1.870%	0.620%	0.380%	–1.490%	–2.240%	0.590%	–1.240%	0.720%	2.090%	0.010%
2003	0.530%	0.090%	0.120%	2.530%	3.230%	1.350%	1.160%	1.660%	0.970%	2.290%	0.940%	1.830%
2004	1.810%	1.140%	0.650%	–1.220%	–0.440%	0.700%	–0.850%	0.120%	1.520%	0.840%	2.700%	1.560%
2005	0.120%	2.020%	–0.860%	–1.530%	0.850%	1.520%	2.290%	1.060%	2.180%	–1.410%	1.920%	2.140%
2006	3.500%	0.610%	1.970%	1.730%	–1.840%	–0.390%	0.020%	0.960%	0.110%	1.800%	1.760%	1.610%
2007	1.130%	0.790%	0.910%	1.590%	2.000%	0.720%	0.370%	–1.450%	2.510%	2.870%	–2.070%	0.520%
2008	–3.260%	1.230%	–2.380%	1.930%	1.820%	–1.730%	–2.100%	–1.210%	–6.990%	–8.410%	–2.800%	0.370%
2009	–0.140%	–1.460%	2.040%	4.270%	5.570%	0.370%	2.970%	1.780%	3.190%	–0.060%	1.330%	1.840%
2010	–0.410%	0.760%	2.820%	1.270%	–3.210%*	–0.930%**						

Source: BarclayHedge Ltd. (www.barclayhedge.com).

* Estimated performance for May 2010 calculated with reported data from 2,828 funds.

** Estimated performance for June 2010 calculated with reported data from 576 funds.

diligence is key. It is something that everyone regardless of pedigree, experience, assets under management, and track record needs to go through before any investment is made. Ask questions and demand answers. If you have questions about due diligence or are looking for information on the credit crisis and hedge funds, email me at das@hedgeanswers.com

A Brief History of Hedge Funds

It used to be that if you queried students at business schools about where they wanted to work after graduation, responses would be names like Salomon Brothers, Goldman Sachs, or Morgan Stanley, as well as General Motors, Coca-Cola, or IBM.

Now, however, students say they want to work for firms like SAC Capital, Maverick Capital, and The Clinton Group—in other words, hedge funds, organizations that were not on the radar screen of Middle America until the near collapse of Long-Term Capital. Still, on Wall Street these firms have always been looked at with awe.

Once considered a small and obscure pocket of the Street, hedge funds and the firms that run them represent one of the fastest-growing areas of the financial world regardless of how the economy is performing. Unlike traditional investment vehicles, which can only make, for the most part, one way bets, hedge funds can go both long and short so they should be able to thrive regardless of market conditions and volatility. In short, these types of investments should always be making money.

To understand how the hedge fund industry evolved, one needs first to understand where the concept came from. First, however let's define what a hedge fund is and how it works.

The term hedge fund was coined by Alfred Winslow Jones, a sociologist, author, and financial journalist who got interested in the markets while writing about Wall Street for *Fortune* magazine in the 1940s.

Jones started the first known hedge fund in 1949 and as such defined the term by his style of investing, management, and organizational structure.

Although Jones is credited with laying the foundation for the industry, many on Wall Street believe Roy Neuberger, the founder of the securities firm Neuberger Berman, Inc., was the person who created the concept of a hedge fund. Others believe it was Benjamin Graham, the father of securities analysis, who devised the method and formula for paying managers.

Regardless, when people think of the history of hedge funds and where they came from, they always think of Alfred Winslow Jones.

The problem is that many do not know about the Jones organization or his investment style or how he defined his hedge fund. In fact, there had not been an article of substance written about Jones for more than 20 years until October 1998, when *Grant's Interest Rate Observer* published a significant story on Jones in the wake of the near collapse of Long-Term Capital.

The industry has changed quite substantially since Jones launched his fund, A. W. Jones & Co. The most important change is to the definition of what he created.

Today the popular press defines hedge funds as private investment pools of money that wealthy individuals, families, and institutions invest in to protect assets and to achieve rates of return above and in fact well beyond those offered by mutual funds or other investment opportunities. For the most part, the press is correct with this part of its definition; however, the problems start when the press uses words like secretive, aggressive, and leverage to describe the actions of hedge fund managers.

Where it errs is in defining the methodology as well as the concept of these private investment vehicles for sophisticated investors.

More importantly, in light of recent industry changes and pending regulations, the hedge fund industry is going to be open to more and more investors. Investors with as little as $50,000 can now access hedge funds either directly or through funds of funds and exchange traded funds.

By the end of 2010 , investors with as little as $10,000 will be able to own hedge funds in their portfolios as new products are being created to give these folks a taste of Wall Street's forbidden fruit. The industry is becoming more and more mainstream as a direct result of traditional long-only managers' inability to put up consistent returns over a long period of time and the simple realization that markets don't always rise and therefore portfolios need to be hedged. Today, retail investors have realized that they need to be both long and short in the market just as Jones did more than 50-odd years ago.

The intricacies of how hedge funds operate as well as who invests in them and why will be discussed in later chapters of the book. The term "hedge fund" is like most things on Wall Street—it sounds tricky, but once it is dissected it is quite easy to understand.

It is my belief from talking to colleagues, relatives, and friends of Jones that he had no intention of creating a product that was difficult or one that would have such a lasting effect on Wall Street and investors.

Rather, I believe he would have wanted the masses to understand his idea of the use of hedged stock positions to minimize risk and would have hoped that it—the strategy—would be employed widely throughout the investing world.

One of the reasons hedge funds operated in relative obscurity until the Long-Term Capital debacle is because of the lack of interest in these products by the press. Prior to 1998, there were very few substantial pieces written about the industry and its role on the Street. Reporters seemed to be afraid of scratching more than the surface about how hedge funds work, but truly enjoyed using the term and people affiliated with hedge funds in headlines for shock purposes and to sell papers. In early 2010, some of the great headlines included "Wall Street's Golden Boy Paulson Loses Some Glister"[8] and "Hedge Fund's 'Terminator' Buy Upheld".[9]

These are simple words and phrases that are used to grab attention with little or no explanation or background. That is okay, after all the headline is supposed to pull you into the story. The problem is the stories do not always do a good job of describing what is happening and leave the reader wanting more.

Fault for obscurity cannot be blamed solely on the press. Many hedge fund managers refuse to talk to the media because of Securities and Exchange Commission rules regarding marketing and solicitation. The SEC does not allow managers to market their funds or to solicit investors that are not prequalified, and talking to the press could be construed as marketing and soliciting. And nobody wants to get charged with soliciting. Still, there is quite a decent flow of information to the media, and news usually gets out. It may not always be the best information and the sources may be questionable but it does get out. That being said, I believe that if the SEC relaxed some of its rules around solicitation and marketing, the information would still be weak and the coverage sloppy. There is a lack of understanding about why talking to the press is important and what benefit it can play in building a business on the part of the hedge fund industry, and as such—rules or no rules—the industry will remain tight-lipped.

For the most part, everyone I asked to talk about their own business and the industry spoke freely and I believe honestly about what they do and how they do it. Also, in the past few years or so, in light of a number of frauds and crises, it seems managers are opening up more. This, in my opinion, can only help the industry.

Since Jones created the hedge fund industry, only three articles have been written about him that have any real merit or worth in my opinion. Two are by the same journalist and ran in *Fortune* magazine, while the third was published in *Institutional Investor.*

To understand how important the articles are to the industry, we first need to understand the Jones model. No matter how far managers today deviate from the definition, each and every one operates with some of Jones's original characteristics.

According to Jones, as described by Carol Loomis in her January 1970 article in *Fortune* titled "Hard Times Come to the Hedge Funds" (still considered to be one of the definitive articles on Jones and the industry), a hedge fund is a *limited liability company* structured so as to give the general partners—the managers—a share of the profits earned on the investor's money. Further, a hedge fund always uses leverage and always carries some short positions. Jones called his investment vehicle a "hedged fund"—a fund that is hedged and is

limited liability company

a legal structure that is the hedge fund investment vehicle.

management fee

fee paid to the manager for day-to-day operation of the hedge fund.

performance fee

fee paid to manager based on how well the investment strategy performs.

protected against market swings by the structure of its long and short positions. Somewhere along the line Wall Street's powers that be dropped the "d."

The method for sharing in the profits is defined in the hedge fund's fee structure. Under the Jones scenario, the managers receive 20 percent of the portfolio's profits—and nothing else. Therefore they have quite an incentive to pick winners and, more importantly, to do right by the investors.

In recent years, managers have added a management fee of 1 to 1.5 percent of assets to the 20 percent performance fee. It is unclear who decided to add this fee, but like most things on Wall Street, when it works, people copy it. This fee basically allows the managers to cover the cost of maintaining the fund's operations as well as providing a bit of a salary. The Jones organization never levied management fees on its partners.

According to Robert Burch, Jones's son-in-law and the current operator of A. W. Jones & Co., Jones never believed in management fees.

"He believed that [management fees] would only breed more assets and take away from the concept of performance and induce the fact that you could make more money building assets than through performing according to the model," says Burch. "Jones was concerned with performance and did not want to be distracted by asset-gathering."

For the most part, the Jones model worked well in both up and down markets, as it was intended to do. In its first 20 years of operation, the system worked so well that the Jones fund never had a losing year. It was not until the bear market of the late 1960s and 1970 that it posted losses.

The hedge fund industry has truly grown very large very fast. It seems that everyone who wants to be in the money management business wants to work for or own a hedge fund. This is not theory but practice, as many mutual fund managers, traders, and analysts are jumping ship to start their own funds. As Wall Street failures mounted and tens of thousands of people were laid off, many looked to starting a hedge fund as a way to get back in the game. These people are setting up entities that they call a hedge fund and—voilà!—they are in the business.

The problem is that many who are calling themselves hedge fund managers are not. To have a hedge fund you have to *hedge*. Therefore, those who do not hedge but call themselves a hedge fund are operating nothing more than a very expensive mutual fund.

Many managers still follow the classic Jones model, using leverage and having long and short positions that allow you to maximize returns while limiting risks in both rising and falling markets. Probably the person who best exemplifies the Jones model today is Julian Robertson.

Robertson, who is discussed in Chapter 2, is considered by most to be the person who took over Jones's spot as the dean of the hedge fund industry. Although his fund organization has evolved quite considerably over the last 10 years, Robertson continues to exemplify what Jones had in mind when he defined and developed his idea.

Robertson, who covered Jones while he worked at Kidder Peabody, built an enormously successful business—Tiger Management—at one time managing in excess of $20 billion. Like most other hedge fund managers, Robertson lost a considerable amount of money in the turmoil of 1998—more than 10 percent of his assets under management—and in the wake of the euphoria surrounding technology stocks opted to shut his funds down and return assets to investors rather than invest in stocks of companies that he "did not understand."

Today Robertson operates a hedge fund incubator, working with new managers to help them build their businesses while actively trading the markets with his own capital. Robertson's legacy is that his organization bred success, and many of the people who passed through Tiger's doors have gone on to do great things in the hedge fund industry. It is estimated that nearly 20 percent of all of the assets allocated to hedge funds are run by someone who formerly worked at Tiger—one of the so-called Tiger Cubs. Although Robertson is known to be an arrogant, egomaniacal hard worker, he is possibly the greatest money manager of all time and quite a gentleman.

"Julian is the natural successor to Jones," says Burch. "He has built a business around the principles and disciplines that Jones used to build his business. He understands the Jones model and uses it to make superior returns regardless of market conditions."

The Current State of the Hedge Fund Industry

It is impossible to get an absolute number of how many hedge funds exist or the exact amount of assets the industry as a whole has under management. The numbers of both change as fast as you can make telephone calls to people who track this information. The SEC requires mutual funds and corporations to report financial information quarterly, which makes these data literally just a click away.

With hedge funds it is not so easy. There is no regulation or requirement for fund managers to report data. Many fund managers are quite happy reporting data when profits are up; but as soon as things go south, the information does not flow so freely. Often, a fund manager also ignores the tracking companies when the fund reaches investor capacity and can no longer accept investment dollars from outside its current group of investors. In this case, the fund manager no longer needs the tracking service, because new investors will only have to be turned away.

For the purposes of this book, I am going to define the size and scope of the industry as follows: There are over 10,000 hedge funds with $1.6 trillion in assets under management at year-end 2009.[10] In 1971, an SEC report on institutional investors estimated that hedge funds had $1.06 billion under management.[11] At the time, the SEC found that Alfred Winslow Jones's organization had just under 23 percent of all of the assets under management placed with hedge funds.[12] Hedge fund industry data is not hard to come by—there are many sources—however, because there is no requirement that managers report performance or assets under management data to a single source, many including myself question the quality of that data. That being said, Table 1.3 details assets under management since 1997, which clearly shows the trajectory of the hedge fund industry.

Today, a hedge fund can be any sort of private investment vehicle that is created as either a limited partnership or a limited liability corporation. In either case, the vehicle falls under very narrow SEC and Internal Revenue Service (IRS) rules and regulations. Hedge funds are limited as to how many investors they can have, either 100 or 500 depending on their structure and on the types of investors they can accept into their portfolios. The structure also determines the type of investors it can accept, either accredited or superaccredited.[13] Institutions that include nonfinancial companies are able to invest in either type of fund.

Beginning in 1998, in the wake of LTCM, Congress and other U.S. officials have begun pressing for more controls and monitoring systems for the industry. For the most part, little if anything of substance had been done to increase regulation prior to 2004.

In the fall of 2004, the SEC voted to require all hedge fund managers with 15 or more investors and $25 million or more in assets under management to register as a Registered Investment Advisor. The ruling was adopted by the SEC and put in place effective February 1, 2006. The idea behind the regulation was that, once registered, the fund manager would come under the authority of the SEC similar to the way mutual funds are regulated by

TABLE 1.3 Hedge Fund ($ Billion)

	Hedge Fund Industry ($B)
Dec-97	$ 118.23
Dec-98	$ 143.10
Dec-99	$ 188.90
Dec-00	$ 236.61
Dec-01	$ 321.92
Dec-02	$ 505.45
Dec-03	$ 825.64
Dec-04	$ 1,228.96
Dec-05	$ 1,360.71
Dec-06	$ 1,713.10
Dec-07	$ 2,136.83
Dec-08	$ 1,297.21
1st Qtr 2009	$ 1,171.87
2nd Qtr 2009	$ 1,169.43
3rd Qtr 2009	$ 1,205.57

Source: BarclayHedge Ltd. (www.barclayhedge.com).

the commission. However, the regulation was challenged in court by Phil Goldstein, and he won. The rule was done away with, and the SEC refused to reinstate it or something like it. Since the collapse of two Bear Stearns hedge funds and the ensuing credit crisis and financial meltdown, Congress has been actively working on developing some sort of laws to regulate this so-called unregulated industry. However, as of this writing, nothing has been put in place, and it is believed that nothing will be put forth until after the midterm elections. There has been much written about Goldstein and his victory. One great story appeared in *Fortune* magazine titled "The Man Who Beat the SEC." It is worth a Google.

The reason many of Wall Street's traders and would-be traders are flocking to set up and work for hedge funds is because the industry is considered by some to be the last bastion of capitalism.

"When we started, it was very difficult to get through the paperwork and raise capital," says Jim Rogers, who was George Soros's partner for more than 10 years. "Now it is very easy and people specialize in setting up the funds and raising capital. It is probably the most efficient way to make money in the financial world."

Rogers's sentiments are echoed in an article about hedge funds that appeared in the popular press. The article describes a number of start-up funds and their managers. Why do they leave their soft jobs at white-shoe investment firms to go out on their own? The answers: freedom and money.

According to one article, written by Bethany McLean of *Fortune* magazine, "No other career in finance gives you the freedom to be your own boss and invest in anything, anywhere, that gets your juices flowing," or provides these people with the opportunity to "get so rich, so fast, so young."[14]

McLean quoted one manager's quip: "I can wager your money on the Knicks game if I want."[15] This is true, it is legal, and it is very, very scary.

A number of former Jones employees have said that many of these people would not have been able to work for their company nor to succeed in the markets in which the Jones organization thrived. Clearly statements like the one above were not what Jones had in mind when he developed hedge funds.

Still, to understand this and where the idea of a hedge fund came from as well as how the business was born, one needs to learn about the father of it all.

Alfred Winslow Jones—The Original Hedge Fund Manager

Alfred Winslow Jones started what has come to be known as the first hedge fund in 1949. His basic investment strategy was to use leverage in combination with long and short sales in order to hedge risk should the market turn against him.

Jones, who died at the age of 88 in June of 1989, devised a formula for the vehicle while researching a freelance article for *Fortune* titled "Fashion in Forecasting," which ran in the March 1949 issue. To research the piece, he spent many hours speaking with some of Wall Street's great traders and brokers. Upon learning their methods, he devised his own ideas on investing based around the concept of hedging—something very few people did in those days. And so with three partners he launched the fund at the age of 49.

"My father took a very long time to find himself," says Anthony Jones, one of Jones's two children. "He graduated from college with some of the same loose ends that many people who graduate have today and basically tried a number of things before he realized what he wanted to do."

After traveling the world on a tramp steamer as purser, he believed he had found himself when he joined the Foreign Service.

"He was in Germany in the early thirties and watched the rise of Hitler and then was assigned to Venezuela, and the prospect of going from Berlin to

Venezuela was so depressing that he quit the Foreign Service," Tony Jones says. "He came to the United States and got involved in sociology."

Jones's interests in sociology and the idea of how social movements developed led him to enter Columbia University. He earned a Ph.D. in sociology in 1941, and it was at Columbia that he met Benjamin Graham.

"His graduate work was interrupted by my parents' marriage, and their honeymoon took them to civil war Spain," says Tony Jones. "In Spain they did a survey for the Quakers—neither of them carried a rifle or drove an ambulance—and toured around with interesting people reporting on civilian relief."

Upon returning to the United States, Jones took a job with *Fortune*, where he worked until 1946. Whether he knew it or not, it was here where he would be laying the groundwork for a lifetime career.

After leaving *Fortune*, he worked as a freelancer for it and other magazines, writing on social and political issues as well as finance. The research and reporting Jones did for "Fashion in Forecasting" convinced him that working on Wall Street was not as difficult as many believed.

"He would come home every day while he was reporting the piece and tell me that he did not learn anything new," recalled his widow, Mary. "After a while he started working on an idea and finally came up with something he believed would work." Mary Jones died on January 8, 1999, at the age of 91.

The article looked at how stock market behavior was interpreted by technicians of statistics, charts, and trends. The following is an excerpt of the piece:

> The standard, old-fashioned method of predicting the course of the stock market is first to look at facts and figures external to the market itself, and then examine stock prices to see whether they are too high or too low. Freight-car loadings, commodity prices, bank clearings, the outlook for tax legislation, political prospects, the danger of war, and countless other factors determine corporations' earnings and dividends, and these, combined with money rates, are supposed to (and in the long run do) determine the prices of common stocks. But in the meantime awkward things get in the way (and in the long run, as Keynes said, we shall be dead).
>
> In the late summer of 1946, for instance, the Dow Jones industrial stock average dropped in five weeks from 205 to 163, part of the move to a minor panic. In spite of the stock market, business was good before the break, remained good through it, and has been good ever since.

> Nevertheless there are market analysts, whose concern is the internal character of the market, who could see the decline coming. To get these predictive powers they study the statistics that the stock market itself grinds out day after day. Refined, manipulated in various ways, and interpreted, these data are sold by probably as many as twenty stock-market services and are used independently by hundreds, perhaps thousands, of individuals. They are increasingly used by brokerage firms, by some because the users believe in them and by others because their use brings in business.[16]

"I was a young kid at the time the business was started, and I have no recollection of when he stopped going to work at *Fortune* or writing and started going to work for himself," says Tony Jones. "I do have quite fond memories of going to visit him at his office down at 80 Broad Street in the heart of Wall Street."

Jones's model for his fund had a very simple formula. He basically used leverage and short sales to create a system that allowed him to concentrate on stock picking rather than market timing.

According to Tony Jones, he realized very early on that he was not a good stock picker. Indeed, Tony Jones believes that it was this realization that led him to expand the organization, bringing in budding Wall Street stars to run the partnership's money, to the point where it became successful.

"He was a good salesman; he knew people to raise money from, and was a good organizer and administrator. But when it came to picking stocks, he had no particular talent," he says. "This meant that his job was to find people who did have talent."

Working for and with the Jones organization was very lucrative. All partners received a piece of the 20 percent that Jones was paid by the limited partners, and they were able to invest in the vehicle.

Brokers knew that if they had an idea and the Jones people liked it, they could sell it over the phone. One broker told me that he used to like to run all of his ideas by the Jones people before calling other clients. He knew that they would act immediately if they liked his idea, but also would tell him if the situation would not work and in turn helped him from pushing a bad stock.

"These were some of the smartest and savviest investors and traders of the time," the broker says. "They gave you a straight scoop on the situation. It was a lot of fun covering the account."

In addition to developing the hedge fund, the Jones organization perfected the art of paying brokers to give up ideas. Although the firm executed most of its orders through Neuberger Berman, Inc., it paid brokers for ideas. Should a broker call on one of Jones's managers, he knew that if the manager used his idea, he would be paid regardless of where the order was executed.

"When Jones's people got an idea, they would call us and execute the order and tell us where the idea came from," remembers Roy Neuberger. "We would give up half of the commission to the guy who came up with the idea, whether he worked for us or not. At the time I did not think the exchange would let us do it. But they did, no ifs, ands, or buts; it was perfectly all right with them."

Neuberger continues, "For many years, the Jones account was the firm's most important account. But it was more than business. We were friends; both he and his wife were friends of my wife and me, and we socialized together."

Jones's strength seemed to be in people as well as ideas. His organization gave birth to many successful managers.

"There were a whole bunch of people who used to work for my father that went on their own," recalls Tony Jones. "After a while he began a business of farming the money out and created a sort of hedge fund of hedge funds."

"Jones made no attempt to pick stocks; he was an executive," says Neuberger. "He understood how to get things done and how to find people to execute his ideas."

One former Jones employee told me that the hardest part of working for Jones was actually getting the invitation to work for him. Jones used a number of techniques to tell the good from the bad, one of which was a paper portfolio program.

"In order to work for my father you first had to prove yourself," Tony Jones says. "To prove yourself, you needed to manage a play portfolio of stocks over a period of, say, six months or so. Every day, you had to call in your trades to the firm and they would be 'executed.' It was only after my father was able to watch how the manager was doing with the play money that he invited them in as partners."

The firm tallied up the profits and losses and examined not only how well the prospective managers performed but also how they did it.

"When it came to hiring managers, my father was very cautious," Tony Jones says. "He wanted to know how they operated and watched very carefully to see what types of decisions they made with the play money. If everything worked out, they got a job."

Another interesting point of the Jones organization was that he did not fire people. If you performed poorly, he simply did not give you any more money to manage and took pieces away little by little so eventually there was nothing left. And the manager had to leave.

From all accounts, Jones was very satisfied and proud of his invention and he appreciated the publicity that he received. Yet he was not very interested in talking about money or the stock market.

"Jones was not a man who was very interested in Wall Street or making money; rather he was interested in the intellectual challenge of it all," says son-in-law Burch. "Although he made a lot of money, he was not very interested in spending and gave a lot of his money away, creating things like the Reverse Peace Corps and other foundations to help people here in the United States."

Jones was very involved with a number of charitable organizations in New York City. One cause to which he was a major contributor and in which his son and daughter are still quite active is the Henry Street Settlement.

Founded in 1893 by Lillian Wald on Manhattan's Lower East Side, the Henry Street Settlement provides programs that range from transitional residences for homeless families and a mental health clinic to a senior services center and a community arts center.

"My father liked to travel to Third World countries. He liked to have a mission, but he had a notion that a number of nations criticized the United States for not doing enough to help out on their own shores and that drew him to Henry Street," remembers Dale Burch, Jones's daughter. "He liked the fact that it helped the community from within itself."

Jones also created an operation called Globalization for Youth, an antipoverty program that used a number of resources to keep children from getting into trouble.

"These are the types of things we talked about," says Tony Jones. "He was very concerned with family solidarity and all of the theories that evolved in the late fifties and early sixties that are currently social work orthodoxy."

Once he launched his fund, he very rarely talked about what he did or how he did it. "When you had dinner with Jones, you always had four or five guys from various parts of the world," recalls Burch. "You didn't know if that night you were going to discuss some pending revolt in Albania or what language they were speaking in Iran.

"It was an interesting challenge to participate in the dinner conversation. The discussion was never about money and never about Wall Street—his mind way beyond that," he continues.

Tony Jones recalls that when the family went to their country home in Connecticut, his mother would drive and his father would go through the evening newspaper with a list of all the stocks his managers had and calculate how they had done that day.

That was the extent to which he brought the business home.

"There was absolutely no time for discussions of what stocks might go up or down at home," says Tony Jones.

Jones did not have many of the characteristics of other Wall Street legends. For example, according to his son, at Christmastime when the brokerages his firm did business with wanted to give him presents, he would accept only items that could be consumed.

"Many of the Wall Street firms tried desperately to give him gifts as a thank-you for all of the revenue he generated, and he would never accept anything except for something he could eat in the next week," Tony Jones recollects.

"We got a Christmas turkey from Neuberger Berman but when it came to gold cuff links or the like, forget about it."

Roy Neuberger called Jones a thinker, not necessarily a hard worker, a sentiment that seems to be echoed by his son.

"My father's entire life was preoccupied with ideas, some crazy and some not so crazy," Tony Jones says. "He had the capacity to read a book and then just get on the phone and call the author up and have lunch. He got to know people and many things and was constantly thinking about everything under the sun."

According to Tony Jones, after his father read a book claiming that the works of Shakespeare had been written by the 16th Earl of Oxford, he decided that the theory was sound and talked about it for two years.

"After his journalism days, and getting in the business, he did not really have long-term interests," Tony Jones says. "He was more interested in things he could focus on short-term. The idea of tackling big projects was not something he was interested in."

Beside countless articles, Jones did publish one book, *Life, Liberty, and Property,* in 1941, based on his doctoral dissertation. According to Daniel Nelson, a history professor at the University of Akron, it was the rarest of dissertations: technically sophisticated, engaging, and addressed to a general audience. A new edition of the book was published in March 1999 by the University of Akron Press.

Although most of the articles written about Jones say he had planned to write a second book, his son says he wanted to but "it would have been a monumental task." When Jones retired from the hedge fund business completely in 1982, he was satisfied with the business but not with it being his life's work.

"Later on in his life, he wanted to write a memoir but could not focus himself on getting it done," Tony Jones says. "There was nothing about running his business that required real concentration—it was a brainstorm kind of thing, and he was good at it."

Jones did not simply hit an age and retire. Rather, he started to give up his duties at the firm and eventually turned the reins over to Lester Kissel. Kissel, a lawyer from the firm Seward & Kissel and an original partner in A. W. Jones & Co., assumed control for a few years. Because of conflicts over the direction of the organization, he was asked to step down, and, after a brief stint by Jones, Burch took over. Today Burch and his son run A. W. Jones in New York City as a fund of funds.

"My father was not at the top of his game when he turned things over to Kissel," says Tony Jones. "Kissel was a lawyer, not a businessman. He never did anything intentionally to harm my father, but he did hurt the business."

By today's standards, Jones did not become extraordinarily wealthy from the business. Still, he spent the bulk of the money he did have on charities, not on lavish living.

However, one of Jones's great loves was his 200-acre estate in Connecticut that allowed him to enjoy the outdoors.

"My father was a landscape visionary," says his son. "He was always trying to figure out things to do with water and moving land around.

"His mind was all over the place," he continues. "Everything he did, did not require an enormous amount of steady follow-through on his part. He had a lot of good ideas and made them reality."

Tony Jones believes his father's reason for switching from journalism to Wall Street was that he wanted to live comfortably, and he knew that he could not achieve that as a journalist.

"He had carved out a unique niche for himself writing but realized that he would never be able to live the kind of lifestyle he wanted to being a journalist," says Tony Jones. "My father was also determined to find out if his crazy idea would work."

Although most people point to the research for the *Fortune* article as the genesis, a number I talked to seem to think a combination of things led him to the hedge fund concept.

It is quite clear that while Jones was studying at Columbia he had many conversations with Graham and learned investing strategies from him. This may be where the seeds of the idea were planted.

Jones did know another Graham follower, Warren Buffett, and the two lunched together from time to time.

"The principles of the hedge fund were clearly developed and created by Alfred. However, some of his investment strategies may have come from his discussions with Buffett and Graham," says Burch. "He was the first to put the ideas down on paper and then actually put them to use."

Jones defined the three principles of hedge funds as follows:

1. You had to be short all the time.
2. You always use leverage.
3. The manager receives a fee of 20 percent of all profits.

"It was the combinations of shorting, the use of leverage, and the fee structure, which is how Jones defined what a hedge fund was all about," says Burch.

Jones believed that by aggressively picking long stocks and neutralizing market swings by also being short, he would be able to put up extraordinary performance numbers while reducing risks.

At all times, Jones's funds maintained a number of short positions that would enable them to have a hedge against a drop in the market, which limited his downside exposure. It is impossible to get a complete accounting of the fund's track record because of the private nature of its activities and investors.

According to Jones's *New York Times* obituary, in the 10 years prior to 1968 the firm had posted gains up to 1,000 percent. It is estimated that the Jones fund had over $200 million under management at the end of that period.

Soon after that, however, things began to not go very well and the Jones organization, like many other hedge funds, took a serious hit. By year-end 1970, the Securities and Exchange Commission estimated that the fund organization had a mere $30 million under management. It is unclear exactly where the money went, but some was lost to market mistakes and the rest vanished as partners pulled out.

Interestingly enough, the only fund the SEC tracked during that same time period that did not see a decrease in assets was Steinhardt Fine Berkowitz & Co., headed by the soon-to-be-legendary Michael Steinhardt.

By 1977, when the hedge fund industry had plummeted from over $2 billion to roughly $250 million under management, many in the industry thought the concept had seen its day.

Jones himself was quoted in an article in *Institutional Investor* in May 1977 as saying, "I don't believe it [a hedge fund] is ever going to become a big part of the investment scene as it was in the 1960s. . . . The hedge fund does not have a terrific future."[17]

Indeed, as with all things associated with the markets, hedge funds had been going through a rough time; but the cycle soon righted itself. Slowly but surely, through the late 1970s and the 1980s, the industry got back on its feet. It was the bull market of the 1990s, however, that really put hedge funds on the map.

Today the combination of shorting and going long in stocks is second nature to even the most immature Wall Streeter, but 30 years ago it was a daring concept.

Loomis, in her piece "Hard Times Come to the Hedge Funds," wrote that her previous story on hedge funds, "The Jones Nobody Keeps Up With," inspired some people to start their own funds, using "the article about Jones as a sort of prospectus, relying on it for help in explaining, and selling, the hedge fund concept to investors."[18]

Slowly but surely, Jones is continuing to get the recognition he deserves. Whether people realize it or not, and I think most do, Alfred Winslow Jones, the sociologist and businessman, created one of Wall Street's most important concepts. His invention gave life to thousands of entrepreneurs and has made and will continue to make many people very wealthy for years to come.

Chapter 2

How Hedge Funds Operate

This chapter explores how hedge funds operate and the role that these investment vehicles play in keeping markets moving around the globe.

It is important to understand how to start a hedge fund, who is investing in the vehicles, and who provides services to the industry. It is here that you will read about "the world's greatest investor" and how he came to get this title.

The sport of blaming hedge funds for financial meltdowns was never more apparent than in the summer and early fall of 2008 when volatility rocked the world's markets and the walls seemed to be truly tumbling down. The near collapse of the global financial system was splashed across newspapers around the globe, and hedge funds were both a victim and cause of the global disaster. Blaming hedge funds was not new, reporters and editors had found a scapegoat for any financial disasters that occurred since the near collapse of Long-Term Capital Management (LTCM) in 1998. Hedge funds are blamed for all that ails the markets—regardless of if it is true or not; if something bad happens, it's the hedge fund industry's fault. The table was set for the blaming of hedge funds for the recent credit crisis but the press needed to put a name and face on the destruction and in turn moved away from hedge funds to focus on Wall Street chief executives, the head of retail banks, and of course the mortgage people. It had looked for awhile as though hedge funds had dodged this bullet; however, that was not the case, and by mid-2008 hedge funds were once again getting the blame.

It's easy, and it does make a lot of sense, to blame hedge funds for all that ails the worlds' financial markets. First, most of them shun publicity and refuse to speak on the record about their strategies or investments. Second, many global organizations, including the International Monetary Fund (IMF) and the World Bank, not to mention the Securities and Exchange Commission (SEC), the Federal Reserve System, and central banks around the globe, have trouble tracking hedge fund operators' moves and do not seem to be comfortable with the way these money managers seem to operate. Lack of information and understanding makes it easy to target and to point a finger when all hell breaks loose and markets begin to collapse.

So why shouldn't society blame such secretive organizations for its financial woes? I don't have an answer. It makes sense to me. When problems strike, why not blame those who are doing well, because surely their success comes at the expense of others, right? That is the view of many of the leading financial journalists—particularly the print people at newspapers in New York and London. Thankfully, cooler heads prevail—at least sometimes.

To understand why blaming hedge funds for every currency crisis and drop in the Dow Jones Average is downright silly, we first need to look at who is operating and investing in hedge funds and why.

Many of the hedge funds that were once blamed for wreaking havoc on the world's markets were whacked quite hard during the recent financial crisis and were wiped out.

It was just a matter of time, said one fund manager I spoke with in September, who believed that woes of the firms like Bear Stearns and Lehman Brothers were just the tip of the iceberg, and that by year-end 2008, there would be more carnage then anyone could have imagined in the so-called smartest area of money management. The hardest hit, he believed, would be the hedge funds, and he was right.

"People are not interested in losing money," he said. "The whole reason why investors go with hedge funds is because they want superior returns but also want to be protected when the markets get shaky. Losing half of your assets is not the type of protection that most people have in mind—hedge funds that don't hedge are going to be wiped out."

While many funds did fail, investors have not lost total faith in the hedge fund industry. The blood has been cleared from the streets, and the hedge fund industry has recovered and survived.

The events of 2007 and 2008 were not unique, the hedge fund industry had been hit before; the late summer of 1998, the tech bubble of 2000, and the bear market of 2002 displayed a lot of the same characteristics of the 1970s and early 1980s when hedge funds also experienced hard times. However then, like now, the industry righted itself, and went on a tear, posting very strong returns and attracting many investors and imitators. To understand how the industry evolved we need to go back in time.

For most of the 1950s and 1960s, many people copied and tried to imitate Alfred Winslow Jones and his staff's method of investing and trading. They wanted to emulate the Jones model, which used a series of long and short positions to put up very significant returns. This strategy worked until the *bear market* started in 1969, when these investment partnerships took it on the chin; most of them eventually went out of business.

The *Fortune* magazine piece titled "Hard Times Come to the Hedge Funds," by Carol Loomis in January 1970 captures the essence of the hedge fund phenomenon and its explosion. At the time, Loomis estimated that 150 funds around the country had assets under management totaling $1 billion. The hook of the story was that many of the fund managers had not seen 1969's bear market coming. In fact, some funds, including A. W. Jones's, had been negative or flat for the year, causing many of the fund managers to change their strategies and reevaluate their business models. A few went out of business altogether.

bear market

a prolonged period of falling prices.

Jones's two partnerships each finished 1969 down over 30 percent for the year, while the New York Stock Exchange composite was off 13 percent.

One of the most interesting points of Loomis's article is revealed in Jones's comments that the problems of 1969 were predicated on Wall Street's "craze for performance" and that "money managers … got overconfident about their ability to make money."[1]

One needs only to look at other recent articles in the mainstream press about hedge funds to see that the same sort of euphoria is sweeping the industry today. In the past 10 years, their numbers have exploded. Since 1990, the assets that hedge funds manage have grown tenfold while the number of hedge funds has ballooned at approximately the same rate.

Some people estimate that a new hedge fund opens every day and believe that until the *bull market* bubble truly bursts and enough people get badly hurt, there will be no end to this trend. One person close to the industry told me that the best thing to happen to hedge funds is that Wall Street is having problems.

"As long as firms continue to lay off people and pay significantly smaller bonuses, the [hedge fund] industry will continue to be strong," he said. "If you lose your job, what could be easier than setting up a fund? And if you get a small bonus, you think that you can do it yourself and don't need anyone."

bull market

a prolonged period of rising prices.

As history tells us time and again, the market is about cycles. Hedge funds are not going to be wiped out completely, but it is inevitable that once the bull leaves the ring, a number of them will vanish and the explosive growth in the industry will subside. If some of the biggest, smartest, and most powerful funds took such huge hits from technology, Russia, and Asia, prudent thinkers have to believe that others will go down as well. The industry experienced this sort of pullback in 2008 and early 2009, yet it has bounced back quite strong in early 2010. New funds are launching, assets are being raised, and hedge funds remain the envy of Wall Street and of course the evil that men do.

"It is very simple. A lot of people follow the herd mentality. Right now the herd is going into hedge funds," says one hedge fund manager who requested anonymity. "Eventually, the herd gets wiped out; this is what happened in 2008."

Starting a Hedge Fund

Today pretty much anyone with $50,000 to $100,000 in operating capital can start a hedge fund. In terms of assets under management right out of the box, one needs at least one to five million to get the fund off the ground. The most important character traits needed are an ego, an entrepreneurial spirit, guts, and the ability to manage money. A track record also helps, but in some cases experience is frowned upon, particularly if the person comes from the mutual fund world. It is very difficult for a manager to raise significant assets without some sort of track record or pedigree right out of the gate. In most cases, institutional investors—pension plans, endowments, and insurance companies—like to see at least three years of performance before they invest with a manager. Most funds launch with friends and family money out of the gate; as such a track record is not necessary, and relationships are more important.

The use of the money mentioned above is for legal expenses, operating expenses, and other sundry items that come up when launching a business.

A budding hedge fund manager needs somewhere between $25,000 and $50,000 to cover the costs of the legal work. There are some firms that will do it for more, there are some that will do it for less; this is a ballpark figure in the spring of 2010.

The key to choosing the right lawyer is to hire one who has experience in creating the type of fund you want and who is not going to be learning on your nickel. It is also important to choose a lawyer with a good reputation in the industry and one who is recognized by investors—using a lawyer not recognized for his or her expertise in the industry is an objection many investors use to say no to you when you ask for your money. The hedge fund legal marketplace is full of good, competent, and well-regarded lawyers. If you need help with a lawyer, email me at das@hedgeanswers.com

Legal fees and operating costs are important to have covered before you set up your fund; however you also need investable capital. It is more important to launch a fund than it is to wait around for the capital to come in and then launch the fund. What I mean is that, over the course of the year, I probably get between 50 and 100 requests from people saying that they are "going to launch" a fund and can I give them some advice. My answer is always the same: launch the fund and get started. Even if you have $100,000 on day one, it is one more day of track record that you will have under your belt. Waiting for money to come in to launch is something of a fool's errand in my book.

The launch number is different for every manager. Some managers start with as little investment capital as $25,000, while others jump out of the gate with millions or even billions in assets under management. More in this case is better than less, but what is most important is that you get started.

Once the entity is created and a brokerage account is opened, the manager is in business. Crossing that bridge is the hardest, most important, and the beginning of something. So do it. Don't wait.

The advances in technology in the past few years have made gathering investment ideas as easy as picking up the phone and clicking a mouse. Many would-be A. W. Joneses are setting up shop in their living rooms, basements, or attics, installing computers with dedicated Internet connections and placing trades immediately.

One manager told me that it is much more efficient to trade out of his apartment on Manhattan's Upper West Side than from an office in midtown or downtown. He doesn't have to waste time commuting, and he can work no matter what time of day it is without the hassle of riding the subway. He knows the rent, he is comfortable in his surroundings, and he can avoid the noise and distractions of an office—not to mention the expense.

"I no longer need to be on the ground in every country I want to invest in, nor do I have to worry about reporting accounting or brokerage functions because of the strides made in technology in the last few years," says the manager. "Most of the initial information I need is available on the Bloomberg or the Web, and by having a personal computer hooked into both, the information is literally a click away. Technology allows me to get the process started a lot quicker and makes the investment process a lot more manageable. It allows me to kick the tires of more companies faster than ever before."

"Kicking the tires" is a theme that many of today's up-and-coming managers employ when they go after investment ideas—it is something that had been lost with the technology explosion in the late 1990s, but in 2010 it is something that all but the black box traders are doing in one way, shape, or form.

Prior to the technology explosion, if you wanted information on companies in Senegal or on stocks in Australia, you needed to be on the ground in the country or wait until your broker opened an office there to get information. Today, the speed at which information travels provides managers access to news and research 24 hours a day, seven days a week, 365 days a year. You now can not only get a quote on any stock anywhere in the world, but you can also get a map on how to get there by pointing your Web browser to a site and clicking the mouse. With Google maps, you can practically sit at your desk and watch people move in and out of a warehouse, production facility, or market—actually getting on a plane, while not defunct has been reduced.

Paul Wong, the former manager of Edgehill Capital, constructed what he called "Hedge Fund Heaven," an office off the entryway of his home in Connecticut where he managed his portfolio and handled all fund operations just a few steps from his kitchen and where his kids played.

In his slice of heaven, Wong installed a series of ergonomically correct workstations, along with requisite computers, phone lines, and fax machines. He also had a couch and a television with dvd player.

"Having the office in my home allowed me to run a business and be an active father," he says. "I could go to my kids' Little League or tennis matches and then come home and check my positions. I was able to work productively at things that were important to me."

Wong believes the convenience allowed him to be not only a better father but a better manager, too. "I can work whenever I want," he said. "I literally can put my kids to bed and be in the office in five minutes looking at reports or scouring the news. I no longer have to carry tons of paper around in a briefcase or spend hours commuting."

Technology is just one thing that has helped the hedge fund industry. Another is the explosion of those who provide services to the hedge fund community. Whether it be law, prime brokerage, administration, accounting, capital introduction, or something else, they are literally everywhere and ready, willing, and able to help you launch and maintain your business. While the community of hedge fund service providers is quite big—as is the case throughout much of Wall Street—many of the industry's players, including the managers, lawyers, accountants, administrators, and brokers, know each other. Still, as the industry grows it is impossible to keep track of all of the providers offering services to both new and existing hedge fund managers.

"It used to be that everyone literally knew everyone in this business," says Bill Michaelcheck, chairman of Mariner Investments, a hedge fund organization profiled in Chapter 3. "Now because everyone and their brother is starting a fund, it is getting harder and harder to know everyone and, more importantly, to know what everyone is doing."

An interesting twist is that many of the marquee names who have been at the forefront of the hedge fund world for decades are slowing down and setting up their children in funds.

Take, for example, Jack Nash, who retired in 1997 from Odyssey Partners and set his son up with a new fund called Ulysses. Michael Steinhardt, who had been threatening to retire for many years, finally did so in 1995, but he has a son who is running his own fund. In October of 2004, George Soros announced that his two sons, Robert and Jonathon, would become deputy chairmen of Soros Fund Management, which at the time had over $12 billion in assets under management.

According to an article called "The Other Soros" in *Institutional Investor* in March 1998, Robert Soros said he had no pressure or encouragement from his father to enter the business. Rather, George Soros felt it would be hard for Robert to work in a place where his father cast such a big shadow. It would seem that the shadow is fading.

Slowly, over the last decade the patriarchs of the hedge fund world have passed the torch to the next generation, who no doubt will work very hard to continue the legacy created by their parents.

It was not always as easy to start a hedge fund as it is today. Fifteen years ago, it would have been hard to find a lawyer or accountant who could help. Of course, many knew of the investment vehicles and understood the structure but very few specialized in the industry. That picture changed with the success of the business and many flocked to it, not only as potential fund managers but as supporting players.

Today, many of the main figures in the hedge fund industry work together, and through a network of referrals you can find some of the best legal and financial talent available, usually with one phone call. It takes just one phone call to schedule an appointment with an accountant, a lawyer, and a prime broker, and from there 60 to 90 days to launch a fund.

"The idea is to provide as much service as we can to the manager in order to make sure we are able to get and hold on to the business," explains an employee at one of the leading prime brokerage firms. "Although hedge funds are a dime a dozen, the key is to work with funds that are going to grow and be successful so that over time the business grows from within instead of relying constantly on new clients."

Many of the service providers, attracted by the industry's exponential growth, market their organizations as one-stop shopping sources for all the fund managers' needs. At conferences and seminars, prime brokers team up with lawyers who are connected to accountants who work with third-party marketing agents, all in the name of service and, of course, the generation of fees for their respective businesses.

Experts ascribe the growth of hedge funds to the acceptance by the investing public of alternative investments and to the fact that people in general have more dollars to invest.

"There are many people who have a lot more money today than a few years ago, and they are looking for better returns than they can get in mutual funds or individual stocks," says a fund manager who recently retired and requested anonymity. "The strength of the economy [prior to the financial collapse] has not hurt the industry. When people make millions of dollars through stock options and initial public offerings, eventually they realize they have to do something with the money if they want to hold on to it. And what they want to do with it is invest in hedge funds."

"Sure, they can put it in mutual funds or individual stocks, but they would rather put it into something exotic that may pay better returns and give them something to talk about at cocktail parties," he continued. "And besides, anyone can buy a mutual fund or stock, only a relatively few can invest in hedge funds."

As the market grows, people are looking for investment opportunities that are unique and that will provide them with greater returns while managing risk and leverage. The ability of a hedge fund to use any means necessary to post excess returns makes it very attractive both to investors and to potential managers. The excess return or Alpha is the difference between what you get investing in an S&P 500 index fund and an actively managed hedge fund. There is upside and downside potential, however, and true or not, people believe that there is greater upside potential then downside potential and are willing to make the investment.

Over the past few years, a number of independent studies have shown that, on average, hedge funds post higher rates of return than those of the S&P 500 and other benchmarks. This ability to continually outperform the market appeals to potential individual investors who are looking for higher returns and are not concerned necessarily with the accompanying higher risk associated with hedge funds. Institutional investors are also focused on actuarial tables and as such need products that will deliver. Many believe that the only way to get to where they need to be is by using investments that can take advantage of all the arrows in Wall Street's quiver.

Still, there are naysayers who believe hedge funds' ability to outperform the market is overstated. It comes down to choosing the right manager. In short, due diligence....

Tables 2.1 through 2.3 illustrate hedge fund performance versus both equity and fixed income indexes. The charts show performance numbers for funds with various trading styles and strategies for the period from 1997 through mid-2010. The data was compiled and supplied by Barclay Hedge Ltd.

TABLE 2.1 Barclay Hedge Fund Index Historical Data

	Jan	*Feb*	*Mar*	*Apr*	*May*	*Jun*	*Jul*	*Aug*	*Sep*	*Oct*	*Nov*	*Dec*
1997	3.620%	1.180%	–0.990%	0.490%	4.060%	3.110%	4.700%	0.520%	4.050%	–1.270%	–0.190%	1.290%
1998	–0.190%	3.760%	3.540%	1.150%	–1.680%	0.230%	–0.460%	–7.810%	1.050%	2.170%	3.780%	2.950%
1999	2.230%	–0.840%	3.480%	4.920%	1.150%	4.130%	0.820%	0.320%	0.740%	1.900%	5.330%	7.730%
2000	0.950%	6.760%	1.740%	–1.470%	–1.000%	3.260%	0.060%	3.740%	–0.710%	–1.070%	–2.520%	2.200%
2001	3.040%	–1.440%	–1.110%	2.020%	1.470%	0.510%	–0.570%	–0.180%	–2.580%	1.840%	2.020%	1.710%
2002	0.660%	–0.480%	1.870%	0.620%	0.380%	–1.490%	–2.240%	0.590%	–1.240%	0.720%	2.090%	0.010%
2003	0.530%	0.090%	0.120%	2.530%	3.230%	1.350%	1.160%	1.660%	0.970%	2.290%	0.940%	1.830%
2004	1.810%	1.140%	0.650%	–1.220%	–0.440%	0.700%	–0.850%	0.120%	1.520%	0.840%	2.700%	1.560%
2005	0.120%	2.020%	–0.860%	–1.530%	0.850%	1.520%	2.290%	1.060%	2.180%	–1.410%	1.920%	2.140%
2006	3.500%	0.610%	1.970%	1.730%	–1.840%	–0.390%	0.020%	0.960%	0.110%	1.800%	1.760%	1.610%
2007	1.130%	0.790%	0.910%	1.590%	2.000%	0.720%	0.370%	–1.450%	2.510%	2.870%	–2.070%	0.520%
2008	–3.260%	1.230%	–2.380%	1.930%	1.820%	–1.730%	–2.100%	–1.210%	–6.990%	–8.410%	–2.800%	0.370%
2009	–0.140%	–1.460%	2.040%	4.270%	5.570%	0.370%	2.970%	1.780%	3.190%	–0.060%	1.330%	1.840%
2010	–0.410%	0.760%	2.900%*	1.280%**								

Source: BarclayHedge Ltd. (www.barclayhedge.com).

* Estimated performance for March 2010 calculated with reported data from 2,767 funds.

** Estimated performance for April 2010 calculated with reported data from 647 funds.

TABLE 2.2 Barclay Equity Long/Short Index Historical Data

	Jan	Feb	Mar	Apr	May	Jun	Jul	Aug	Sep	Oct	Nov	Dec
1997	3.740%	0.160%	–1.090%	0.120%	5.080%	2.930%	5.790%	1.370%	5.890%	–1.030%	–0.700%	1.510%
1998	0.120%	4.660%	5.390%	1.760%	–1.200%	0.950%	–0.490%	–6.920%	2.870%	2.740%	3.400%	4.380%
1999	3.490%	–2.130%	3.690%	5.570%	1.270%	4.040%	1.420%	0.110%	1.060%	2.470%	7.620%	10.990%
2000	0.610%	9.860%	1.070%	–2.260%	–0.450%	3.480%	–0.590%	4.730%	–0.350%	–0.930%	–2.550%	3.300%
2001	2.650%	–1.520%	–1.140%	2.030%	1.320%	0.290%	–0.550%	–0.530%	–2.670%	1.420%	1.720%	1.970%
2002	0.380%	–0.580%	1.800%	0.380%	0.500%	–1.850%	–2.870%	0.230%	–1.600%	0.500%	2.090%	–0.660%
2003	0.060%	–0.620%	–0.050%	2.160%	3.170%	1.370%	1.640%	2.000%	0.470%	2.410%	0.810%	1.430%
2004	1.690%	0.860%	0.730%	–0.970%	–0.470%	0.770%	–1.210%	–0.360%	1.490%	0.370%	2.290%	1.240%
2005	0.340%	1.760%	–0.500%	–1.710%	0.940%	1.610%	2.350%	1.090%	2.110%	–1.290%	1.880%	2.430%
2006	3.230%	0.120%	2.410%	1.200%	–2.360%	–0.540%	–0.310%	0.790%	–0.260%	1.420%	0.940%	1.230%
2007	1.030%	0.700%	0.800%	1.240%	1.930%	0.930%	0.150%	–1.160%	1.630%	1.990%	–1.860%	0.350%
2008	–2.790%	0.840%	–1.870%	1.740%	1.840%	–0.920%	–1.710%	–0.620%	–4.920%	–3.760%	–1.030%	0.890%
2009	0.220%	–1.410%	1.290%	2.870%	3.800%	–0.090%	1.720%	1.880%	2.230%	–1.020%	0.680%	1.520%
2010	–0.400%	0.610%	2.120%*	1.420%**								

Source: BarclayHedge Ltd. (www.barclayhedge.com).

* Estimated performance for March 2010 calculated with reported data from 579 funds.

** Estimated performance for April 2010 calculated with reported data from 154 funds.

TABLE 2.3 Barclay Fixed Income Arbitrage Index Historical Data

	Jan	*Feb*	*Mar*	*Apr*	*May*	*Jun*	*Jul*	*Aug*	*Sep*	*Oct*	*Nov*	*Dec*
1997	1.260%	0.670%	1.160%	1.980%	1.590%	0.860%	1.490%	1.010%	1.620%	0.690%	0.350%	0.990%
1998	0.020%	1.070%	1.510%	0.960%	0.360%	0.490%	0.960%	–1.990%	–2.320%	–4.670%	2.610%	2.000%
1999	3.240%	2.230%	1.910%	1.470%	0.360%	0.580%	0.410%	–0.160%	0.710%	1.040%	1.220%	1.380%
2000	1.700%	1.240%	0.800%	0.620%	0.590%	0.930%	0.970%	1.090%	1.040%	0.340%	0.850%	1.000%
2001	1.540%	0.490%	0.710%	1.120%	0.680%	–0.380%	0.310%	0.470%	0.490%	1.140%	–0.290%	–0.360%
2002	0.640%	0.150%	0.270%	1.200%	0.530%	0.140%	–0.500%	0.180%	–0.790%	1.780%	1.820%	1.490%
2003	1.060%	0.680%	0.640%	0.810%	1.230%	0.870%	0.300%	0.610%	0.970%	0.780%	0.580%	1.080%
2004	0.950%	0.200%	0.130%	1.270%	0.660%	0.690%	0.580%	0.230%	0.090%	0.510%	0.700%	0.900%
2005	0.430%	0.580%	0.310%	0.420%	–0.130%	–0.070%	0.730%	0.330%	0.820%	0.550%	0.190%	0.470%
2006	0.700%	0.240%	0.880%	0.960%	0.670%	0.150%	0.650%	0.030%	–0.140%	0.840%	0.340%	0.580%
2007	1.170%	1.520%	0.480%	0.600%	0.290%	–3.270%	–0.590%	–1.300%	1.840%	1.180%	–2.230%	–0.170%
2008	–0.120%	–0.200%	–5.640%	1.520%	1.900%	0.430%	–1.110%	–0.220%	–4.180%	–13.550%	–3.270%	–3.180%
2009	0.170%	0.160%	–1.060%	0.830%	2.460%	1.940%	2.180%	1.880%	4.230%	2.550%	1.220%	1.770%
2010	1.910%	0.260%	1.550%*	2.400%**								

Source: BarclayHedge Ltd. (www.barclayhedge.com).

* Estimated performance for March 2010 calculated with reported data from 40 funds.

** Estimated performance for April 2010 calculated with reported data from 9 funds.

Veterans of the industry often question the excitement surrounding hedge funds and point to the fact that many of today's managers prior to 2008 had never seen a down market or experienced significant volatility. These old-timers question the newcomers' ability to handle the market when it corrects itself.

"It is too easy for people to get into the industry," says Jim Rogers, president of Rogers Holdings and a former partner of George Soros. "When we started out, it was a lot harder and there was nobody around to help us. Now there are brokerage firms, law firms, and accounting firms all specializing in hedge funds, which makes getting into the business easy."

Michael Steinhardt, who had more than 30 years of stellar performance managing hedge funds, disagrees with Rogers in that he believes hedge funds *always* have been an easy business to get into.

"How many other businesses are there where with just a few years of experience you can hang out your shingle in a relatively unregulated industry and get 20 percent of the upside on other people's money?" he asks. "Ease of entry into the business is extraordinary. It always was but it was a psychic leap for people in the sixties and seventies to invest in hedge funds. Today, everybody wants to run a hedge fund and everybody else thinks they should be investing in one."

What has lowered the barrier in the past 10 years is that Wall Street understands how profitable providing services to the hedge fund community can be. The issue now is what happens to the industry now that there is so much capacity and the industry is no longer growing as rapidly as it had in the past; the supply has overcome the demand.

"Starting a hedge fund is probably the most efficient way to make money in the financial world today," Rogers says. "The problem is once things start to turn, people will lose money and things will get ugly, and when they get ugly, everyone loses."

Today, there are more than three dozen organizations I would recommend that will assist potential fund managers in drafting legal documents, providing brokerage services, and marketing and money raising. (There are probably hundreds in reality).

What makes the whole industry so incestuous is that even when people blow up or self-destruct, they can still find work in it and often are able to profit handsomely from their mistakes. More likely than not they will come back either as money managers or in the form of other cogs on the gears that make the industry spin.

When Victor Niederhoffer's operation blew up in October 1997, people said he would never manage money again. The evening after the morning he was shut down, I was at an industry function talking to one of his investors who, prior to the collapse, had been one of his staunchest supporters. The investor told me that he had never seen anything so ugly, and not everything had been fully disclosed.

"This mess is so big, I don't think he will ever be able to work in this industry again," the investor said. "Nothing can save him."

However, saved he was. Four months later the following ad ran in the *Wall Street Journal's* help wanted section:

Financial Markets

> Wanted: Individual with good quantitative mind, creativity, programming skills and interested in aspects of financial markets to work in a small, innovative, formerly successful trading firm in CT. Must be flexible and willing to learn. Low starting salary, excellent potential. Fax resume to Victor Niederhoffer....[2]

The man who prided himself on reading no newspaper other than the *National Enquirer* was back. But, how? How was it possible to have lost so much and yet come back so quickly? The answer is one part ego, one part stamina, and one part rich friends.

Niederhoffer had proved to be a solid money manager. Like a number of people in the industry today, he insisted on making his story known; he wrote a book, gave many interviews, and was available to anyone who would listen to his story. He was known as someone who could bet heavily on one side of the market only to be wrong and then miraculously recover—a wild trader who performed well in any market condition. He also had some very wealthy friends, or, more accurately, one very wealthy friend: George Soros. It seems that unlike most other areas of Wall Street where you are only as good as your last trade, with Niederhoffer it did not matter. Through his connections he was able to reestablish himself and begin trading again. Niederhoffer would not comment on where the money for his current fund came from, but many in the hedge fund world believe a good portion of it came from Soros.[3]

Another money manager who blew up after losing almost all of her partners' capital by betting on micro-cap stocks has found a niche for herself on the marketing side of the business. After a bit of time spent soul-searching, she set up a firm in midtown Manhattan that specializes in third-party marketing of hedge funds, which means she is helping them to attract investment capital. She works within a network of wealthy individuals, family offices (limited partnerships or limited liability companies), and institutions, helping them decide where to put their money.

"Most hedge fund managers I have met and worked with have two problems when it comes to raising money: Number one, they have no interest in marketing, and two, they don't know how to do it," she says. "My experience in both raising money for my own fund as well as having worked in institutional sales has allowed me to build a network of potential investors that are interested in finding a good manager who has a good strategy and who will provide them with solid returns. I believe that I bring strength to both sides of the equation—I know how to pick good managers, and I know how to find money."

Both of these cases illustrate that there is life after death in the hedge fund industry. The Long-Term Capital case presented earlier proves that if you know the right people, you may not have to find work after you blow up.

Before you can blow up, however, you need to create an organization.

There are four essential puzzle pieces to every hedge fund: money, a lawyer, an accountant, and a prime broker. Recently a fifth has been added, an administrator—however, an administrator is not essential to launch a fund. So for now, let's go with the four items above.

Once you find a lawyer, the next item on the list is usually a prime broker, the financial firm that you use to execute orders and manage the money. Prime brokers provide almost everything a fund manager needs to get started—technology for trade and execution services being the most important. In the beginning the accountants are the least important piece of the start-up puzzle but quickly become the most important after the first year of operation. It is at year-end when the accountant prepares the audit of the fund's performance. The audit can be one of the most important tools in helping funds raise money and grow. And an accountant makes it all official. It is also important to note that prior to having the documents go live, you should have an accountant review them in order to make sure the math works. The reason you want the math to work is to make sure that you can get paid, and sometimes the language regarding how fees are calculated is not as clear as it should be or just does not make sense and in turn makes things quite difficult. A quick review is a smart move.

As for money, it takes surprisingly little to get started and through the first year. Most fund managers start out with having enough money in the bank to cover living expenses for a year or two, plus what they have invested in the fund, and some for administrative expenses. The idea is to not worry about where money is coming from to pay bills and live while building a business.

One fund manager told me that she waited for almost two years before she launched her fund to make sure she had enough to cover living expenses for at least two years.

"I knew it would be a very long time before I would be able to take out any of the money I earned in the fund and live on it, so I knew I had to have a lot of money in the bank to ensure it was not a problem."

She also wanted to make sure that she didn't need any money she did earn from the fund to live, so that she could invest it right back into the fund and continue to increase her stake and assets under management.

Some of the most significant costs of doing business are those associated with administering the fund. Administration costs range from data feeds and execution costs to rent and telephone bills. Many new fund managers try to keep these expenses down by working with a prime broker that will provide all the services as part of a package.

However, hedge fund hotels that were all the rage in the 1990s are not as popular today due to issues regarding costs and expenses associated with using the facilities. There still many opportunities to set up shop inside a suite of offices operated by prime brokers, but it is just as easy to set up a stand-alone office—the choice comes down to cost.

Once the fund is up and running, though, many managers build elaborate office complexes and install large organizations to run and administer the operation.

This is in direct contrast to A. W. Jones, who was often ridiculed by his partners and employees for not wanting to spend money on a large office filled with modern accoutrements.

Prime brokers provide the up-and-coming as well as the established hedge fund manager with everything from execution services and daily profit-and-loss statements to analytic and execution systems that can sit on any desktop or laptop machine.

The prime brokerage business in the wake of the credit crisis has gone through a significant transformation. Gone are many of the marquee names who either where shut down, went bankrupt, or just stopped operating. The new thing is the mini-prime—a firm that acts as an introducing brokerage firm for larger firms who don't want to work with small or start up funds.

The prime brokerage map has changed quite a bit in the last two years, but there are still plenty of firms offering the services, and, have no fear, if you want to launch a fund, there will be many who vie for your business.

Success breeds success, operating a hedge fund can be very lucrative to the fund's manager; being the prime broker to a successful fund can be very lucrative to the Wall Street firm providing the services. Wall Street values the prime brokerage business.

Since the early 1990s, providing prime brokerage services has been known as Wall Street's diamond in the rough. The idea is very simple. The brokerage firm provides the hedge fund manager with execution, custody, and clearing. The fund manager and the prime broker have an understanding: The manager will route some of his or her trades through the prime broker's trading desks, which in turn will generate commissions. There is no written agreement that says this nor is there a requirement as to how many trades must be sent to the brokerage firm. That would be illegal. There is, however, an unwritten rule, and managers know that if the prime broker does not see some commission dollars, they will be asked to take their business elsewhere.

Most prime brokers like to see 20 to 30 percent of its clients' commission dollars. If a customer does not send at least 20 percent of its trades to the prime broker's order desks, the manager will be asked to look elsewhere for a prime broker.

Remember, it is very easy for the prime broker to keep track of the fund's trades and where it executes the orders because the firm keeps its books and records. Today, most managers, use multiple prime brokers who then report the daily activity to a broker who creates reports that detail the activities of the fund and its assets. On any given day at any given hour the firm acting as a prime broker can look at screens and see which funds are trading with it and which are trading away and immediately determine which relationships make sense and which do not simply based on the volume of activity and the commissions that are being charged for the execution of orders.

"It used to be that when you signed on a new client, you broke open a bottle of champagne," says one person who has been in the prime brokerage business since the mid-1980s. "After the crash of 1987, the business took off and has never been the same. There used to be a just a few of us, now it seems like everyone is in the business. But it works, and funds are always launching."

The reason the hedge fund business exploded in the early part of the new millennium was that many on Wall Street realized that their careers and, more importantly, their bonuses were tied to the actions of others. They came to believe it was not worth the risk of losing their jobs because someone else made a mistake or because of the rogue actions of a few. Running a hedge fund, at least in the beginning, you have just one person to blame if it does not work out: yourself.

"By opening up hedge funds, people could be their own boss and know that they did not have to worry about how others performed," says one industry observer. "They just had to rely on themselves and not some pencil pusher in operations or in the counsel's office who thinks they know something about making money."

Today the prime brokerage business represents a significant piece of revenue for many firms. Goldman Sachs, for instance, which for years said it would not work with managers who were just starting out or who managed only a small amount of assets, has changed that policy and will now work with almost anyone; and, if they for some reason do not want the business, they will refer the fund manager to a mini-prime who acts as an intermediary to Goldman. Goldman gets the business; it just gets routed through a different source instead of coming directly to the firm.

The reason why everyone is willing to work with the start-ups is because nobody knows where the next Soros, Robertson, or Steinhardt will come from. And the brokerage firm does not want to miss out on potentially huge sources of revenue that may come down the road from funds that grow and succeed and in turn pay the company large commissions.

In the past few years, many of Wall Street's biggest and smallest brokerage firms built their prime brokerage business to the point that it is hard to tell one from the other. Entire franchises are based on technology, especially the order execution systems. All reporting and analytical functions are at a manager's fingertips via the Internet.

Not only do the prime brokerage systems store current data, but they also provide historical information. The systems are designed so that a manager does not have to wait for reports to be delivered or to have documents retrieved to get a picture of the fund's situation. Technology has been the great equalizer in the prime brokerage business.

Prime brokerage is such a profitable business that pretty much all of the large, medium, and small firms offer services to budding and existing hedge fund managers. Over the past few years, many firms have been launched to simply provide hedge fund managers with just execution services. One- and two-man trading companies that use third-party software and clear their trades through the large clearing houses are now offering services to budding and existing managers. These shops specialize in order execution at very cheap prices, which means that fund managers can save money on commissions; and by clearing the trades through brand name firms like Goldman, Pershing, and Penson, the clients can say they work with the best and brightest firms.

And while smaller shops have opened and gotten into the game, larger firms are continuing to expand the products and services that they are offering to hedge fund managers. It used to be that you needed to have significant assets to get into some of the "name brand" prime brokers; now, however, as long as you have some money under management, pretty much any of the firms will open an account for you. The business is so lucrative that firms including; Fidelity Investments, the large mutual fund company, offers prime brokerage services to the hedge fund community.

Today, because the hedge fund industry is growing at such a fast pace even in the wake of the credit crisis, there is plenty of business to go around; and most firms operate under the unwritten rule not to poach clients. However, in recent years as the market has turned, funds have gone out of business and the pace of new fund launches has slowed; there are some firms that have declared it open season and are aggressively pursuing the clients of other firms.

"Our business is a safe bread-and-butter business that allows the firm to profit handsomely for providing services while taking very little risk," asserts a person in the prime brokerage industry. "We have never had a situation evolve where we lost money or took a capital hit when a fund blew up. The most we can ever lose is commission dollars. If a fund blows up, we will replace it with another."

Just to be on the safe side, in light of the blow-up of many funds in 2007 and 2008 and armed with the lessons of Long-Term Capital, many firms have begun to aggressively reevaluate their risk exposure to make sure that they do not have too many funds with concentrated portfolios that could pose a risk to the firm's business. According to one prime brokerage executive, the firm's management committee did not understand the services and function that its prime brokerage unit provided to its hedge fund clients and was nervous about the "risks" it was taking in this line of business.

"I have been called a number of times by senior management requesting information about what sort of risks we were taking and losses we should expect when the market turns or a hedge fund blows up," said a risk manager at a large prime broker in New York City, who requested anonymity. "When I told them none, they first questioned if I knew what I was talking about and then thanked me for doing my job so well."

Technology has not only been good to prime brokers, it has been good to the hedge funds; as such, no longer does one need such a big infrastructure or organization to be in business and—more importantly—make money. While hedge fund hotels still exist, these sort of operations are not as widely used as they were just four or five years ago. That being said, there are still many office suites around the major cities of the world that are littered with hedge funds.

In one room you may have a fund that specializes in special situation equity plays; in another you may find a manager who trades foreign currency options, while a third may simply trade small-cap equities that are linked to the financial services industry. Each has a different strategy and management style, yet some may have the same investors.

Prime brokerage services are just a small part of what is often thought of as a sophisticated world of hedge fund operations. In reality, like most businesses, the fundamentals of operating a hedge fund are quite simple.

In most cases there are just three aspects to the business: marketing and raising capital, legal and accounting work, and investing and trading. Most managers do not want to have anything to do with the first two and therefore farm them out to third parties. In the past few years, managers have found they can pretty much get all of their trades executed and their legal work and accounting functions handled by outsourcing at a fraction of what it would cost to do them in-house.

Most hedge fund managers have no interest in marketing and, more importantly, don't have any idea to how to do it, which is why they hire third-party marketers. The third-party marketer's job is to find investors. The marketers promote the fund and its manager to everyone from wealthy individuals and family offices to corporations, endowments, and pension plans in a clear, succinct manner. Third-party marketers are paid a fee for bringing in capital, and the revenue streams remain for as long as the investor's assets remain at the fund. In most cases the marketing firm works on an exclusive basis just as a real estate broker would if you were trying to sell your home. However unlike real estate, there is no multiple listing service in the hedge fund industry. Raising capital is the single hardest thing to do for most managers. Most believe that if they build it, the assets will come; that is simply not the case. Once a manager realizes that people don't care about their funds, they look for internal and external marketers to help raise assets. Both can be extremely lucrative. However, in the last few years, the third-party marketing business or placement agent business has come under a lot of scrutiny by the State Attorneys General of New York and Connecticut and as such seems to be coming to an end. At the time of this writing, there were a number of investigations going on by both of the above-mentioned agencies into how money was raised for both hedge funds and private equity funds.

In today's competitive marketplace the key to survival is the ability to attract and keep investors. To do so, a manager must put up solid returns quarter after quarter, and the marketer must be able to tell likely investors a compelling story.

Many managers run into a catch-22 when it comes to attracting new investors. In most cases, new managers have very little track record of their own, and therefore they do not have much muscle behind their story. While traders may have been successful at Goldman or even other hedge funds and received huge bonuses, who is to say what they will do on their own or how much of their success was based on their own effort? Therefore, managers who strike out on their own need to have a large group of contacts and character witnesses who can bring potential investors to the table.

A recent trend in the industry is that of large, established hedge funds and money management firms placing investment dollars with start-ups. These are called emerging manager platforms.

One fund manager I spoke with had been approached by a number of the hedge fund world's marquee names offering to invest in the new fund. At first the manager could not believe the good fortune. But this situation had a number of strings attached. When the manager sat down with the potential investors' representatives, it turned out the hedge funds wanted to wield a lot of control over investment decisions and wanted to split all of the new fund's fees.[4] The manager decided that although it would be great to have their money in the fund, it would be better in the long run to do without it.

"They wanted too much control and I did not think it would be worth it," the manager explains. "In the short run it would have been nice to have their money, but over time it would have been a problem. It was very difficult to walk away from their money, but looking back I am glad I did."

Many large hedge fund organizations like to give money out to new and smaller managers because they believe it will help them significantly with their performance and also help them with idea generation. The idea is simple; there are just so many hours in a day and only so many good ideas that one organization can find, but, by farming out some of their money, the large manager is able to expand his or her reach in the marketplace and cast a wider net in search of investment ideas and avoid slippage.

"The new fund managers get a good chunk of money that allows them to get established while we usually get the best years of their performance," he says. "And it helps us avoid slippage." Slippage is the losses that a fund manager creates when he or she tries to move large sums of money in and out of a small position and the market moves before the order is completely executed.

It is very hard to move large sums of money in and out of good investments. A manager who likes a stock that is thinly traded needs to be careful that going in or out does not cause the market for the stock to move significantly. Often even the rumor of a hedge fund's going into a stock can cause market turmoil. Therefore a big fund becomes limited as to what it can and cannot buy. It is a lot easier to find places to invest smaller amounts of money, so by putting money with a new fund, a large fund is able to capitalize on situations that otherwise would not be available.

For the most part, once a manager takes money from another manager, there is a confidentiality agreement that does not let the manager who is receiving the money speak about the fund that is providing it. Of course, as long as it does not appear in print, most managers are willing to give up the name to potential investors because it is a pat on the back. If George Soros or Julian Robertson likes this guy and has given him money, why shouldn't you?[5]

"Many large hedge funds spread the dollars around in order to continually put up strong numbers, and in most cases it is good for young managers who can get these investments. The problem is they can't tell anyone about it," says an industry observer who requested anonymity. "If the world knew that some of the largest funds were doling out money to people who were still wet behind the ears, how do you think that they would react when the performance comes in and they have to pay such a large percent of the profits to people who did not even do any work?"

Regardless of the outside investors, the most important aspect of a start-up fund is the manager's own stake. Even established funds would have a hard time raising money if the manager did not have a significant stake in the fund. Investors are saying to the managers, "Put your money where your mouth is."

A hedge fund is doomed if managers do not have their own money in it. It really does not matter how much, but some managers put every penny they have in their fund.

One manager told me that at one point he was putting so much into his fund that the gas and electric company were threatening to cut off service to his home. His office assistant finally persuaded him to take some money out of the fund to live on, but he says it was difficult because he believed so strongly in what he was doing that he wanted to have as much invested as possible.

As hedge funds continue to become more popular, many future Wall Streeters are going right into business for themselves instead of working for a brokerage firm or hedge fund. Everyone who has ever made a few bucks in the stock market believes that they can be a hedge fund manager. With some regularity, I get emails from high-school and college kids who want to start a fund using a personal account of $25,000 or $50,000. And while I applaud this excitement and interest, it is not realistic; one needs to work and have some experience or at least a high-school education before they get into the business and really make a go of it.

One fund manager started his fund while in high school and ran it through four years of college. He told his investors that he would be closing the fund and would liquidate all of its positions by year-end and return their capital. He wrote in his annual letter to investors: "After serious thought, I have reached the inescapable conclusion that I will not be able to work for somebody else and simultaneously manage [the fund]. After graduation I must just join the real world and find gainful employment."

I wonder if the manager's investors knew he was not in "the real world" while he was investing their "real money" in "real securities," and that, although he had "real gains" he could instead have had "real losses."

Most hedge fund managers understand that they operate in the real world and that their real careers are on the line based on their investment decisions. This is not always the case with those who cover the industry. The popular press is often quick to criticize managers because they are apt to make a deal when it comes to accepting new investors.

Nobody is forced to invest with a manager. An individual or institution does it by choice. In all cases it is up to the investor to perform due diligence and determine if the manager's investment ideas and criteria mesh with his own investment objectives.

An article in *Forbes* in April 1998 questioned one manager in particular because the minimum investment in his fund was "negotiable" and because he ran the fund out of his apartment in Manhattan.[6]

The same article also questioned famed hedge fund operator Julian Robertson for having lowered his minimum investment to $1 million from $10 million and for requiring new investors to sign an agreement not to withdraw their money "for five years, even if Robertson 'goes insane, dies or becomes incapacitated.'" The story did not mention, however, his stellar track record for the previous 20-odd years or his continuing ability to reinvent his investment strategies. That's what allows him to take advantage of the world's ever-changing economic landscape.

Hedge Fund Regulations and Structures

When Loomis wrote her *Fortune* article, she looked at some of the people who were investing in hedge funds. As can be expected, a list of names was very hard to come by, but she found a who's who of the nation's rich and famous. It includes Laurence Tisch, Daniel Searle, Keith Funston, Deborah Kerr, Jimmy Stewart, Jack Palance, and Rod Steiger. Today the lists of investors (which are even harder to come by) also read like a who's who of the nation's rich and famous as well as pension plans and endowments from all 50 states.

One hedge fund investor who should be noted is Laurence Tisch. A very savvy businessman, he has had not such good luck with picking hedge fund managers. Although he refuses to comment on whether he still invests in hedge funds, it is widely known that he is an investor in John Meriwether's Long-Term Capital through a company he owns. It is believed that when he heard of the firm's losses, he immediately asked for a redemption of his investment and wanted to extract what little money he had left.

Neither Meriwether nor Tisch would confirm this story, nor would Tisch comment on his investment practices. An article in the *Wall Street Journal* revealed that Tisch did have some money invested in Long-Term Capital through Loews Corp. The article says that the Tisch exposure to Long-Term Capital was a result of its purchase of Continental Insurance of New York in 1995. The insurance company had invested $10 million in Long-Term Capital in 1994, and it received a payout in December 1997 of approximately $18.25 million. The company kept $10 million in the fund and saw that get marked down to under $1 million when Long-Term Capital collapsed.[7]

It is also widely known that Tisch did have substantial positions in a number of hedge funds in the 1960s and 1970s that went belly-up. At the time, he was quoted as saying he'd had it with the hedge funds.

My alma mater, Clark University, is an active investor in hedge funds. According to James Collins, the university's executive vice president for administration and finance, Clark has been investing in hedge funds since 1993. "The university's investment committee decided to invest in hedge funds because we wanted to diversify our risk exposure and work with some of the smartest minds on Wall Street."

Clark has approximately 20 percent of its endowment invested in several hedge funds, all of which use different investment strategies. To find the fund managers, the university relies on a number of existing relationships its board of trustees have with Wall Street. Members of the University's board of directors sit on an investment committee that meets regularly with university officials and consultants to review, monitor, and evaluate both funds that are in the portfolio and potential investments.

"The program is working as we thought it would, and we expect to continue seeing absolute returns of 10 percent to 11 percent from the investments," Collins says. "Over time we believe it will prove to be the right investment for the university's money."

In the fall of 2004, JP Morgan Securities Ltd. released a study titled "Have Hedge Funds Eroded Market Opportunities?" The study looked at the significant growth in the hedge fund industry over the past few years and questioned whether the size of the industry eliminated a manager's ability to find opportunities to exploit in the market. The study concluded that in areas such as fixed income arbitrage and long/short equity there has been an erosion of opportunities as hedge fund managers scramble to find places to deploy their capital. It did find that opportunities existed in areas where few hedge funds were willing to roam, including the credit and foreign-currency markets. Nonetheless, the study found that it was "too early to write off" hedge funds. The industry did not do well in 2004 as most funds put up barely positive returns through the first ten months of the year but did quite well in the last two months—postelection euphoria. And although hedge funds may or may not offer an opportunity to investors, the industry is still growing at a significant clip. JP Morgan found that through the period of 1990 to 2003 the industry increased fourfold from 2,000 to 8,000 funds. The industry's assets during the same period grew 20 times, from $38 billion in 1990 to $817 billion at the end of 2003. According to Barclay Hedge, a well respected tracker of the hedge funds, the industry had more then $2.1 trillion in assets under management at the end of the second quarter of 2010. Hedge funds regardless of the what the pundits say are here to stay.

Although these numbers seem impressive and represent significant growth in comparison to the traditional side of the investment management business, they are not so big. For example, at the end of 2003, the amount of money invested in the world equity and bond markets was close to $74 trillion. On this basis, hedge fund assets represent just two-thirds of 1 percent of the total assets in the market.

Investor money comes from all sorts of sources today: college endowments, state pension funds, municipalities, corporations, family offices, wealthy individuals, and now retail investors. Harvard, Yale, California Public Employees Retirement System, California State Teachers' Retirement System, and The Texas Association of Public Employee Retirement Systems are some of the most famous and respected hedge fund investors on the institutional level.

In the early 1990s, many corporations and other institutional investors shied away from hedge funds because of issues regarding transparency and understanding investment strategies. However, as the industry becomes more mainstream, hedge fund investing is a more essential part of most serious investor's portfolios.

"Hedge fund investors are no longer an elite core of the world's wealthiest investors," says Steinhardt. "Publicity about sustained superior returns attracted hordes of money into funds. But many of the old funds such as mine had high minimums and were closed to new money. That alone created a certain mystique about hedge fund investing."

Now, however, because of the proliferation of information as well as market forces, hedge fund data and resources are readily available through sources ranging from specialized consulting firms to web sites. If you type the phrase "hedge fund" into a search engine on the Internet, it will come up with more than 11.6 million results.

Another factor that is causing hedge fund information to be more readily available is the change in the regulations surrounding the number of investors.

In 1996, the National Securities Markets Improvement Act quintupled the number of investors allowed in hedge funds to 500. Since hedge funds began in the late 1940s, the total number of investors allowed had been 100. Sometimes fund managers and their lawyers interpreted the law so they could have only 99 investors because they also counted the general partner as a limited partner. However, according to Richard Valentine, a former partner at the law firm of Seward & Kissel, the general partner did not need to be counted.

"People thought that they had to count the general partner as an investor and therefore could only have 99 other slots, but, in reality, if they wrote the partnership agreements properly, the general partner did not have to count," he says.

Although the law is pretty clear on limits placed on advertising and marketing—they are not allowed—many fund managers realize that to reap the benefits of the new legislation they need to get their message out. Therefore it is not uncommon today to find an article in the major financial press that touches on hedge funds or focuses on various aspects of the industry. Many managers want to distance themselves from the others and are therefore willing to state their case now more than ever.

A lot of fund managers have also started to become more interested about the world's markets and national economic policies. The Securities and Exchange Commission still does not let hedge fund managers use conventional methods of advertising. Some say this has helped create the mystique of the industry and its managers, while others believe it ensures the safety of unsuspecting investors.

"By not letting fund managers advertise or market their businesses, the SEC has created a veil of secrecy over the industry that really helps the managers attract business," says an industry observer. "People in general are more interested in things that they are told they cannot learn about or do not have easy access to, and therefore it has become easier in some cases for managers to attract investors. People want what others cannot have."

Most of the prime brokers work with their fund managers to help them raise capital through capital introduction services. But because the funds are not allowed to advertise, this process can be quite difficult. Often a brokerage firm will put together a report on a number of fund managers, detailing their strategies and performances but without actually naming the specifics. The firm will also hold seminars, in which prequalified investors are invited to hear manager presentations.

The prime brokerage provides this to its clients to help them market their funds to potential investors and increase their assets under management. Most firms have Cap-Intro meetings that take place either once a month or once a quarter. The events, which are usually a morning or an afternoon, consist of presentations by managers about what they do and how they do it. The idea is to get investors interested in the manager to learn more about the strategy. The meetings are good because a potential investor can literally see four or five managers in an afternoon at one location. In the early part of 2010, the number of Cap-Intro meetings was growing at a very fast pace. It seemed like there was a meeting almost every week in New York and other major financial cities around the globe.

"The process is hard, but it is the only way we have been able to figure out to market the funds without running the risk of running afoul of the law," says a person who markets hedge funds for a prime broker.

The change in the regulations allows funds to expand the number of limited partners they can have and redefines the guidelines under which an investor must qualify to invest.

Prior to the financial reform bill that was signed into law by President Obama in the summer of 2010, the only requirement was to be an *accredited investor*, which is defined as someone who has $1-million net worth, including a primary residence, or an annual salary for two consecutive years of $200,000 ($300,000 for a couple) however, now the requirement does not include the value of the potential investors primary residence. The Dodd-Frank legislation removed the primary residence from counting toward a potential investors net-worth. While there are set rules as to who can invest in a hedge fund, there are no such rules when it comes to minimum investments. Investments can range from as little as $50,000 to as much as $100 million; it all depends on the size of the fund. Now that the regulations have changed to allow for more investors, the minimums have come down.

accredited investor

an investor who meets the Securities and Exchange Commission guidelines required for investing in hedge funds.

The current regulation now allows for 500 limited partners as long as the fund or entity has not accepted any investors who do not meet the qualified purchaser requirements after September 1996. The fund manager has to make it clear in the offering documents that future investors will be limited to qualified purchasers and has to make available to all pre-September 1996 investors the ability to withdraw their investments at net-asset value without penalty.

A qualified purchaser is defined as any trust, natural person, or family-controlled company that owns not less than $5 million in investments, and any person, acting for his or her own account or that of other qualified purchasers,

onshore fund

an investment vehicle that is set up in the United States that is available to U.S. citizens.

offshore fund

an investment vehicle set up outside of the United States and not available to both tax-exempt U.S. investors and non-U.S. investors. taxable assets.

who owns and invests on a discretionary basis not less than $25 million.

"The change in the regulation has been a great thing for large funds that can attract the really high-net-worth individuals and institutions, but for the little guys who can't fill their first one hundred slots, there is no need for this yet," says Peter Testaverde, a partner at the New York-based accounting firm Eisner LLP. "This whole thing is about the [Securities and Exchange] Commission understanding that people with a net worth of a billion dollars do not need the same protection as Joe Retail when it comes to investing."

Hedge funds for the most part operate in a structure that is either a limited liability company or a limited partnership. The manager of the fund is usually a Delaware limited liability company that operates an *onshore fund* for U.S.-taxable investors and an *offshore fund* for non-U.S. taxable investors.

Today lawyers use boilerplate language for hedge funds' investment memorandums, spelling out to potential investors the structure and strategy of the entity, describing its fund manager and the potential risks of investing in the fund. A potential investor needs to realize that the memorandum is designed to protect the fund manager, so it is very important that potential investors perform their own independent due diligence before investing. Reading the investment memorandum is just a beginning.

Still, there are a number of things that are important to look at when reading an investment memo, including lockup provisions, fee structures, and the type of investments the fund manager plans to make. In most cases, the funds lock up money for one to three years and then allow for withdrawals quarterly. Money can be taken out sooner, however to do so the manager will most likely charge a redemption fee. When it comes to explaining what the fund plans to buy and sell—in short its investment strategy—the documents are usually very vague. The documents say things like, "the manager may use his or her discretion to invest in any or all of the following at any given point in time." The memo will most likely list every single type of security, commodity, or futures contract known to the markets in order to provide the manager with latitude. In most cases, though, managers tend to stick to a specific strategy and trade one or two types of securities or commodities. This information is usually found in other areas of the investment memorandum and in the firm's marketing material. The reason for the vague language is freedom. Managers need to have flexibility to invest and to be protected if something should go wrong.

Overall, the best advice for a potential investor is to get help when picking a manager and completing the due diligence process. Often that advice comes from other investors or consultants. One manager told me that he has a husband-and-wife team that comes off as mild and somewhat naive until they start asking questions about the fund and its investment and management style.

"These sweet old nice people become Attila the Hun and his wife as soon as we start talking about money and investment strategy," he says. "A lot of managers think investors are not so smart or with-it, and it is a mistake. If they weren't so smart or with-it, they wouldn't be qualified to invest in hedge funds."

There are many more different groups of investors in hedge funds today than when Jones started out. Some call these investors greedy, but most of Wall Street believes its best and brightest minds are working for hedge funds. If you truly want to beat the market as well as take advantage of various investment styles that are not open to the general public, hedge funds are the only place to put your money, assuming the fund manager meets the investment qualifications that you require.

In most cases, plenty of information about funds is made available by the fund operators and their marketing agents. In addition, a number of analytical organizations track the industry. Many funds have web sites, and managers are often quoted in newspaper and magazine stories. The explosion in hedge funds has also been greeted by an explosion in hedge fund consulting firms. These so-called independent agencies offer potential investors insight into various styles and strategies. The services also provide data and other relevant information on thousands of funds.

In recent years, there have been some questions and a few scandals regarding the independence of a number of funds. Some independent advisers have been accused of not telling potential investors that they have an arrangement with a hedge fund they recommended and that they receive a fee from it for bringing in new investors. It is not the point of this book to say that these advisers are unethical, but I believe it is my duty to warn the reader of unethical practices by some firms. There has been an enormous amount of media coverage in light of the Madoff fraud regarding the conflict of interests between consultants and their clients. It is very important to ask about potential conflicts before you begin the process and make any investment. Do your homework; it is your money.

The best bet in finding a hedge fund is to use someone you know and trust as an adviser. It is up to investors to understand the type of investment they are getting into, and the only way to do that is to get involved personally.

One aspect of hedge funds that is often confusing is the use of offshore and onshore investment vehicles by fund managers. Many managers have both an onshore fund and an offshore fund that operate with something called a "master feeder" fund. This structure allows the manager to pool all of the funds' assets in one vehicle that splits gains and losses based on the assets of its onshore and offshore partners.

If, for example, the onshore fund has $60 million and the offshore fund has $40 million, 60 percent of the profits and losses would go to the onshore fund and 40 percent would go to the offshore fund.

"Using this structure allows the fund manager to make sure everybody gets the same rate of return and that they don't have to worry about entering an order and allocating the proceeds," says Testaverde. "It is a cleaner way of doing things and gives everybody the same results."

Many fund managers use offshore funds—which are defined as entities that are not registered in the United States because they want to preserve the anonymity of their investors and to avoid a number of tax issues associated with having a fund registered in the United States. However, Washington has become wise to this and is working diligently on closing the opportunities that exist for managers and their off-shore funds.

The regulations surrounding hedge funds for the most part end with the number of investors and with the definition of who can invest in the funds. Recent legislation has changed some of the requirements as to who qualifies to invest i.e. is or is not an accredited investor. However, in light of the impending regulation requiring registration, hedge funds will most likely come under much more scrutiny by the SEC and the powers that be in the months and years to come. Yet, it is all very vague, and it can be expected that hedge fund managers will be forced to be audited by the SEC on a regular basis and will be expected to operate within the strict guidelines of being a registered investment advisor; the financial reform bill is a bit vague on who does and does not have to register with SEC. The common thought is that funds with assets of $100 million to $150 million to be registered as investment advisors, put in place as of this writing. For a while hedge fund regulation seemed to be at the top of President Obama and Congress' agenda, however, in light of the weak economy, the Scott Brown victory in Massachusetts, and other setbacks, it seems to be off the table for the time being.

It is hard to define exactly what a hedge fund is because the various structures used around the globe by managers are so diverse. The clearest definition comes from *Merriam Webster's Collegiate Dictionary*, which defines the investment vehicle as "an investing group usually in the form of a limited partnership that employs speculative techniques in the hope of obtaining large capital gains."

One very famous fund manager told me that the only definition of a hedge fund that he had ever read that made sense to him was the one by Carol Loomis published in *Fortune* magazine 30 years ago: "A hedge fund is a limited partnership organized to invest in securities, with a partnership structured in such a way as to give the general partners—the managers of the fund—a share of the profits earned on the money."[8]

Loomis went to great lengths to ensure that the reader could differentiate between a hedge fund and a simple limited partnership that makes investments:

> The structure has three main features: first, the partnership arrangement, through which managers of a fund can be compensated in such a way as to leave them highly motivated to do well; second, the use of borrowed money to obtain leverage, [a] technique permitting the fund to take maximum advantage of a bull market; and third, the use of short selling as a hedge, or protection against the bear market.[9]

What is interesting is that many within the industry as well as those covering it define the hedge fund by its investment guidelines as set forth by the SEC. Rather than understanding how the vehicle operates, many reporters and industry observers choose to define the vehicles by who can invest, not by what they do.

When I met with Loomis in the spring of 1998, while I was working on the first edition this book, we discussed her articles and the lasting effects they seem to have on the industry. She says she finds it surprising that in all this time, people still turn to these pieces for information and ideas on how the industry operates and how to get started in it.

Prior to the market meltdown and credit crisis, it seemed like everybody in New York except the cabdrivers were starting a hedge fund for one simple reason: *money.* However, now it seems everyone wants to work at a hedge fund or company that provides services to hedge funds.

There are a lot of investment professionals who lost their jobs and are trying to find positions at funds because they think that they can make money and not have to deal with the bureaucracy of a large firm—not to mention the fact that the firms don't seem to be hiring.

There is a lot of greed around the hedge fund industry—it comes in three forms: the managers, the investors, and the service providers. People are looking to start, invest, and serve hedge funds because it is where they believe the money is, and they want it. If people were satisfied with the returns of the S&P or the Dow or some other index, not only would there not be so many hedge funds, but there would be a lot less business on Wall Street.

The reason hedge funds will continue to grow in bad times as well as good is the egos that put people on Wall Street. In good times, people don't want to share profits with the house and they believe they can do it on their own; in bad times, a lot of talented people lose their jobs, and they have egos large enough to let them go out on their own.

One of the greatest advantages to hedge funds had been the manager's ability to use any means necessary to find profitable places to put money. Now that a number of the most exciting places have once again fallen on hard times and many hedge funds have lost large amounts of money, the number of people who want to exploit these exotic opportunities may be getting smaller.

When a fund goes from having $300 million under management on Friday to having just under $200 million in assets on Tuesday, it's hard to attract new money, let alone cover the overhead of the business.

How Hedge Funds Use Leverage

One of the industry's problems is that a lot of managers who find themselves in trouble are not using the Jones model and thus are not running true hedge funds. Instead they are running expensive mutual funds—portfolios that are net long and are closet index funds.

Many managers only use short positions sporadically and therefore are not protected when things do not go their way. To be protected when things go bad, a hedge fund needs to have a significant amount of short positions.

Leverage, despite what much of the press thinks, is not a dirty word. Often those who employ a Jones model will use a 70 percent to 40 percent split of long to short positions. Leverage is an important tool that when used properly can boost returns while limiting risk.

A very simple example is the following situation: If a fund is 75 percent long and 25 percent short, the fund is net long 50 percent—a bullish posture in which the shorts have to work three times as hard as the longs. However, through the use of leverage, the same fund could be 125 percent long and 75 percent short, giving the fund, while it is still net long 50 percent, greater protection on the downside. In this example, the shorts only have to work 1.7 times as hard as the longs. This is business-school Leverage 101, and it is something not to be feared, but to be embraced by both fund managers and investors.

Prior to the credit crisis, the hedge fund industry had been flying below the radar screens of the world beyond Wall Street.

Patriarchs of the Hedge Fund World

Over the years, many of the most respected and sought-after hedge fund managers returned capital to investors, stopped accepting new investors, or simply shut down their operations. These managers all came to a point where they believed that either they could not continue to provide the performance numbers that their investors had come to expect or simply believed that they had gotten too big. The situation always seems to be the same: The managers have decided that they will be unable to continue to post superior returns with the sums of money they have and therefore do not want to risk their performance record with too much money to manage.

In some cases, like Michael Steinhardt as well as Jack Nash and the late Leon Levy of Odyssey Partners, the managers decided that there was more to managing money than they were willing to do at that time and that the best thing to do was to close up shop. While others have decided to give back portions of their assets and continue investing as they have for many years to come, these people decided to get out of the business and pass the torch to relatives or friends.

There have also been a number of instances when fund managers have decided that there's so much opportunity out there that they need to get back some of the money they returned, and so reversed course.

One of the most interesting people to have the left the hedge fund community in the past few years is Michael Steinhardt. He got started in the late 1960s with two partners, Howard Berkowitz and Jerold Fine. In the fund's first 14 months of operation it grew 139 percent. By 1970, it had become the nation's largest hedge fund, with over $150 million under management, according to an SEC report on the industry. The report was detailed in May 1971 in a story in *Fortune* magazine written by Wyndham Robertson, the sister of Julian Robertson. Titled "Hedge Fund Miseries," the article says "the fund was the only large fund whose assets rose in the period surveyed by the SEC."

At the time, Steinhardt, Fine, and Berkowitz attributed the rise entirely to performance and not to capital infusion. Other funds, according to Wyndham Robertson, saw a decline in assets under management. Some funds lost as much as 95.4 percent of their assets while others lost as little as 1.2 percent.

In 1995, after more than a decade of threatening, Steinhardt finally called it quits. He said that he did not want to be "an armchair philanthropist" and that he wanted to be active in his pursuits apart from money management. Those pursuits range from horticulture and exotic animals to collecting art and providing ways to pass on secular Jewish values to others through organizations.

Until 1994, his fund had never had a down year. Then his wrong bet on European bonds caused his funds to lose close to a billion dollars in assets under management.[10] At the time he announced that he was closing up shop, one industry observer told the *New York Times*, "He recovered beautifully from 1994, so no one can say Michael Steinhardt quit because he could not cut it."[11]

A $1,000 investment with Steinhardt from inception to the date it closed its doors in 1995 would have been worth $462,224.

Steinhardt, Soros, Robertson, Tudor Jones, Bacon, and a number of others have built their businesses into so-called super hedge funds. They have proved that no matter how large they get or what type of turmoil rocks the markets, they have the ability to make money.

Still, there has been some question in the past few years whether some of these super hedge funds have become more asset gatherers than traders, simply because the management fees (about 1 or 2 percent) they earn for dollars under management are so huge.

At its height, it is estimated that the Soros organization managed nearly $28 billion in assets under management. It earned approximately $280 million in management fees alone, before it was paid its 20 percent of the profits earned on its investments.

In 1998, before the Asian flu, Druckenmiller said that Soros's flagship fund Quantum was up approximately 19 percent. This being the case, the Soros organization's slice of the pie would have been around a billion dollars.[12]

Obviously, the majority of fund managers earn nowhere near that kind of money. But think of it this way: If a fund has between $50 million and $100 million under management and it charges 1 percent plus 20, the manager stands to gross between $500,000 and $1 million just by showing up for work. If managers show up to work and perform, the revenue they can earn from their funds is nearly endless. It is no wonder Wall Streeters are flocking to the hedge fund world.

When the press and others start to question the fees that funds collect, instead of explaining why they should be so high, the fund managers start to perform. As fast as the managers report their numbers to anyone who will take them, the stories switch from complaints about fees to questions about how the managers are able to do so well and regularly beat the market.

Before all the negative stories about Long-Term Capital, one of the most awful pieces of journalism about hedge funds ran in the April 1, 1996, issue of *Business Week*. The article, titled "The Fall of the Wizard of Wall Street—Tiger: The Glory Days Are Over," was about Julian Robertson. In the piece, *Business Week* accused Robertson of not being able to put up good numbers and of viciously attacking his underlings with his hot temper and erratic management style. The article also accused Robertson of not making company visits and not having an active role in the day-to-day management of his funds.[13]

An outraged Robertson responded in two ways. First, he posted solid numbers for the year, beating the benchmark S&P substantially; and second he filed a $1-billion libel lawsuit against the magazine and its editors. In a settlement, which was reached in December 1997, *Business Week* was forced to say that its predictions regarding Tiger's investment performance had not been borne out and that it had made a mistake in reporting that Robertson no longer made company visits.[14]

Business Week did not retract its comments about his erratic behavior. Although the altercation proved embarrassing for the magazine in light of the media debacles of 1998, the incident proved to have a relatively minor effect on Robertson's organization.

Most people believe Robertson's vindication came not through the settlement but rather by the performance his funds achieved. His trouncing of the market's benchmarks seemed to prove that the entire thesis of the article was wrong. His returns of over 56 percent for the year showed the world that not only was he still in the game but he was better than ever.

Other managers have acted similarly when faced with questions about their ability to manage money and the fees they get for doing it.

Michael Steinhardt told me that one of the things that bothered him the most when he retired was the press's reporting that he did not have a "high-water mark," or a clause in the partnership agreement that says if the fund loses money, the manager will not be paid the incentive fee until it recoups the partners' losses. Steinhardt's fund did not have this clause in the agreement, and the press spent a lot of time writing about that fact when he reported that the fund had lost money for the first time and then announced its subsequent closure.

"While it may now be common industry practice to have a high-water mark, frankly there was no such thing as common industry practices back in 1962," he says. "Hedge funds were not an industry like people talk about them today. It struck me as a bit unfair that the only time the high-water-mark issue came up was in 1994, the one year I lost money, 27 years after I started my fund."

Steinhardt says, "There are two sides of a coin. Anybody after a year can leave, and if you stay in when someone is down, you are in essence saying that you believe in the manager. You do not make the judgment based on if the fund manager has a high-water mark or not; you make it based on if you believe in the manager and his investment abilities. My performance record after 27 years in the business stands up as a testament to what I achieved; my business should not have been blackened by some nuance of the partnership agreement."

As many famous hedge fund managers retire and move into more active private lives, a new group of Midas traders is emerging. These men and women are beginning to stake their claim and make their fortune in the industry.

People like Jeffrey Vinik, the dethroned king of the Fidelity Magellan mutual fund, started a hedge fund in 1996 and in his first year made an astounding 100 percent. His fund went from $800 million under management to $1.6 billion. In late 1998, the fund had over $2 billion under management. Many believe his success was made possible because his hands were not tied by regulations that were placed on him when he managed Magellan.

Imagine what would have happened if Vinik had been able to perform as well as the manager of Magellan as he did with his own fund. Not only would there have been a lot more happy investors, but most likely Vinik would not have been able to earn as much money. At Fidelity, he did not earn as lucrative an incentive fee nor did he have such a substantial stake in the fund, while on his own, he had both.

By 2000, Vinik had tired of managing other people's money and decided to close his fund. At the time he announced the closing in the fall of 2000, the fund had grown to over $4 billion in assets under management. During the four years he ran Vinik Partners, launched in late 1996, he racked up a total return of 646 percent before fees versus 110 percent for the S&P 500. In his twelve-year career running money for Fidelity and on his own, he racked up nearly 32 percent for his investors.

Hedge Funds Take All the Heat

Today, both television and print journalists are enamored with hedge funds and with the people who run them. Every time an indicator, be it the S&P 500 or the Thai baht, moves in a direction that is unfavorable to the masses, journalists blame it on hedge funds. In recent years, political leaders have also started to blame hedge fund managers for their countries' market woes.

In 1997 when the Asian currency crisis hit, the first people to be blamed were not the central bankers or the corporate leaders, but the men and women who run private investment partnerships in the United States and abroad. Ten years later, the credit crisis happened because, according to many, hedge funds let it happen.

This was also the case in 1992 when a crisis occurred with the exchange rate mechanism of the European monetary system. It also happened in 1994 when international bond markets went into a tailspin. With each crisis there is blame, and in each case the blame was placed on hedge fund operators. Journalists and government leaders alike blamed hedge fund managers for wreaking havoc for the simple benefit of posting higher returns.

And while over the last few years the press and powers that be have not blamed hedge fund managers for causing crises in the markets, in 2003, the SEC and the Attorney General of the State of New York completed their investigation of a number of hedge funds, finding that they had worked with mutual fund managers to exploit market efficiencies through a practice called mutual fund timing. Once again, hedge funds had been blamed for the ills that occur in the marketplace. This time, however, they were not blamed for destroying market value or attempting to collapse a regime, but rather were accused of taking advantage of arbitrage opportunities that existed only by circumstance. Unlike other scandals that rocked the hedge fund community, this time these managers did not act alone in search of profits but rather were in cahoots with the mutual fund industry, and both hedge fund and mutual fund managers were proved guilty of wrongdoing. Since the mutual fund timing scandal, many mutual fund organizations have been hit with substantial fees and been forced to retire many of their senior executives. In the case of Strong Funds, the firm was forced to sell itself, and its founder, Richard Strong, accepted a lifetime ban from the mutual fund industry and agreed to pay $60 million in fines. His 30-year-old firm agreed to a $115 million fine for its wrongdoing.

It is extremely hard to prove that hedge funds are a cause of these financial disruptions and crisis. A number of studies have been published recently that show that, except in one or two cases, when a hedge fund was blamed for a financial crisis, it was not at fault. Most of the time the hedge fund gets caught in the middle; rather they are blamed because there is no one else to blame. The Federal Reserve's action regarding Long-Term Capital solidified this argument, however, in the most recent market dislocation, no hedge funds were bailed out or even loaned money; the banks of course stepped in to get this help. Hedge funds were left to fend for themselves. Right or wrong, it is what happened.

Case in point: In the summer of 2008, the credit markets were all but frozen solid. Nothing was getting done, and one day seemed to worse than the next. Many people believe it was caused by the errors made by the mortgage bankers and brokers—the Collateral Debt Obligation creators and marketers. Others thought the causes were rooted in lax government controls and the destruction of the Glass Steagal Act during the Clinton Administration, not to mention the Federal Reserve's inability to successfully keep control over the capital markets and interest rates.

In the early days of the crisis, one of the first causalities was a hedge fund operated by Bear Stearns. The fund got hit by the meltdown of the sub-prime market and was forced into liquidation. It was the first of a number of funds, firms, and other entities to fail because of the crisis. For awhile, it seemed that one fund after the other was hit with massive losses, not to mention the banks and Wall Street firms that were devastated by the meltdown. Although these announcements came as a surprise to many and offered a rare glimpse into the profits and losses of some of the world's most successful money managers, for the most part people did not seem to care until they realized that the entire banking system according to then-Treasury Secretary Henry Paulson and President Bush was on the verge of collapse. The only thing to do of course was to orchestrate a massive bailout—to this date, I am not sure if it was right or wrong but I can tell you this— I do not think that the hedge funds are to be blamed for the crisis. The blame rests firmly in the hands of the greed that swept through boardrooms, the lack of government regulation, the government's inability to regulate, and the simple fact that for too long the foxes seemed to be in charge of the henhouse. Unfortunately, nothing in Washington has changed, and the new administration puts Wall Street veterans—that is the foxes—in charge of the henhouses.

George Soros—The World's Greatest Investor

To understand how finance ministers around the globe came to the conclusion that hedge funds are to blame, we need to look at where and when the ill will toward hedge funds started. The finger-pointing started in the wake of the devaluation of the British pound in 1992. It was after this incident that George Soros become known as the world's greatest and most feared investor.

Soros's efforts netted his fund more than $985 million, truly an incredible bet and enough to make him the world's greatest investor. What most people overlook when they discuss this situation, however, is the amount of risk involved in the bet. It is estimated that at the time he put in the trade, he had more than $10 billion at risk. Had he made a mistake, he most likely would have been wiped out. He bet the ranch, and he won.

The story begins in 1990 when Great Britain decided to join the new Western European monetary system. At the time, according to Robert Slater's unauthorized biography, *Soros: The Life, Times, and Trading Secrets of the World's Greatest Investor*, Soros did not think it was a good idea for Britain because its economy was not as strong as the new united Germany's and therefore would be at its mercy.

Under the European monetary system agreement, Britain was to maintain its exchange rate of £2.95 to the German mark. As its economy continued to get worse, the pound faced increasing pressure, but because of the agreement, Britain was unable to move. Throughout the summer of 1992, John Major's Tory government assured the world that the pound would recover and that devaluation was not an option.

Soros, according to Slater, thought this to be nonsense and believed that the situation was a lot worse than the Conservatives thought. By mid-September, the Italians, facing mounting economic pressures of their own, devalued the lira, albeit within agreement guidelines. This was the beginning of the end for the system's ability to determine exchange rates. The actions by the Italians set in motion the trade that has made the name George Soros known in all corners of the world.

On September 15, 1992, Major's government announced that Britain was pulling out of the European rate mechanism and in turn devaluing the pound. The news rocked currency markets around the globe. Traders were sent running to cover their positions in a desperate effort to limit losses. One trader, however, was laughing all the way to the bank. Before the announcement, Soros had sold $10 billion in sterling. When the news broke, his hedge fund racked up almost $1 billion in profit. One trade, one man, one hedge fund…

From that point on, the world has never looked at hedge funds or George Soros in the same way again. The world now sees these once-obscure investment vehicles as forces to be reckoned with—traders who had the Midas touch.

Since that time, there have been many who have tried to take over the mantel from Soros, but none have been able to do so. Of course the industry has many very successful managers, and its story is not complete. That said, Soros reigns the supreme manager; many have tried, none of have succeeded.

Chapter 3

The Managers

To understand hedge funds, one has to understand how money is managed. The nature of the hedge fund industry is such that managers come from all areas of Wall Street and beyond. There is no one career path that a budding manager takes. Managers come from existing investment firms, brokerage houses, exchange floors, and the back office. Managers come from reading a series of books on investments, as former day traders, doctors, lawyers, and cab drivers. The path to the hedge fund industry is not necessarily paved with gold but once one arrives, the gold is there for the taking.

Over the last 15 years, I have met doctors, lawyers, professional athletes, and mechanics who have traded in their chosen professions to launch a fund. In some cases it makes me nervous, while in others I want to get the fund's wire instructions ASAP. The diversity of managers allows for varying models of success.

Some managers launch with next to nothing in assets under management and grow to billion-dollar funds while there have been managers who launched with billions of dollars and fizzled out a few years after they opened the fund.

I believe the recipe for success comes down to three things:

1. Drive/Ambition
2. Conviction in one's ability to manage money and sticking to it
3. A sense of humor

Over the years, I have met literally hundreds of people who call themselves hedge fund managers, and my research, albeit unscientific, shows that to be successful one needs to have all those characteristics. Remember, it doesn't matter if you are the guy or gal who gets the joke or the gal or guy who does not get the joke, as long as you know who you are, you are in good shape. It is the guy or gal or thinks that they get the joke and does not that we need to be careful of and avoid at all costs.

It has been 10 years since the first edition of this book—this is the third. In previous editions of this book, I have profiled managers, some of whom have gone out of business, merged into larger organizations, left the industry, or continued on to achieve greatness. The managers who appear in this edition are those who have graced these pages in the past. The interviews have been updated. For those of you who have read previous editions of this book and wonder where some of the people went who did not make it this go round, I assure, it is nothing sinister, but rather I just decided to not update the profiles. If you have questions please email me at das@hedgeanswers.com—I will respond.

The managers all use different investment styles and I believe are a good representation of the industry. The idea behind choosing these people is to illustrate the depth of talent in the hedge fund world—and to provide examples of how various managers operate their funds and what types of strategies they employ to have solid performance while working to preserve capital.

The following pages tell the stories of these fund managers. A few readers may know some of them, because they have been around for a number of years, but the managers all have one thing in common: They are very good at what they do, in my opinion. I am not recommending that anyone go out and invest in any of them just because they are profiled here. That would be foolish. What I am recommending is that if you are looking to launch a fund or build a business, you should look into how these managers operate.

Although each focuses on a different investment strategy, and their assets range from a few hundred million to tens of billions of dollars, they all have the same goals—to preserve capital, let profits run, limit losses, and live to trade another day.

In the first edition of this book, which was published in 2000, I profiled 10 managers from across a series of investment strategies and styles. Since then, six of the 10 have either gone out of the business of managing money, have merged their funds with other like-minded funds, or have given back all of their client assets and are simply managing their own money in a strategy similar to that used in their hedge funds. In talking to these people it has become increasing clear that although managing a hedge fund is a great opportunity that can provide significant riches, it is also extremely tough.

"I never knew how hard it was going to be when I got started," said one manager who asked not to be identified. "I thought all I had to do was get the documents done, open an account, hang a shingle, and, poof, the money would start rolling in. Boy, was I wrong." This particular manager never had much success raising money, and that, coupled with mediocre-at-best performance, caused him to close his fund after eight years and look for a job. "I never thought I would have to work for someone again," he said. "Now I have to put together a resume, go on interviews, and hope somebody hires me." It has been more than six months since he shuttered his fund, and he has not found a job. "It is really tough out there," he said. "There are a lot of people who are in the same boat as I am and a lot more who are about to get in with us."

There are no hard-and-fast statistics when it comes to how many funds open and close each year, but it is a lot. Any hedge fund lawyer or accountant will tell you that business is better than ever and that it does not look as though there will be a drought of new business any time soon. A lot of funds are going out of business.

One hedge fund accountant told me that more than 30 percent of the funds that his firm audited in 2008 will not be coming back for an audit in 2009. He said that this situation is a direct result of them not being able to raise money and support the overhead that it costs to run a hedge fund in light of the credit crisis and their inability to put up good numbers.

"These people came from good firms, had track records, and in 2009 got wiped out because they could not put up the numbers and nobody would give them additional capital," he said. "Investors got hurt in 2009, and many have still not recovered; managers who did not perform are not getting any of the money."

The credit crisis aside, it seems that whenever the popular press writes about hedge funds, the stories are about either the fund that launches with a bunch of Goldman Sachs or SAC Capital alumni with billions in assets under management on day one, or about a fund that collapsed. We never read about the guy with $2 or $5 million who is struggling to pay bills, hire staff, and manage money and can't do it, so after a year or two he folds the tent and goes home. These stories after all do not sell papers or provide headline-grabbing appeal to the editors.

Most, if not all, of the managers previously profiled have had very successful careers on Wall Street and were doing very well for themselves when they decided to open their own shops. However, a few did get a dose of reality and have since had to look for careers or opportunities elsewhere. In the end they all learned one important lesson: Managing money is hard, and raising money is harder. And it does not matter how good you are at one if you are not good at the other!

In Chapter 4 you will read about third-party marketers who raise money for new and existing funds. This is a service that some managers need to be successful, however, with the new regulation, and investigations, this business has come under enormous scrutiny and is no longer a sure thing for managers to rely on to bring assets into the fund.

So what are managers to do— if the assets do not come in on day one or day 365? The answer is to dig in, develop a plan, be willing to adapt the plan and go with the flow of the market, and, of course, make it work.

Guy Wyser-Pratte—Wyser-Pratte

Unlike many hedge fund managers who operate in obscurity and seem only to cater to their high-net-worth and institutional clients, Guy Wyser-Pratte is truly a man of the people. His fund and the firm that bears his name specialize in risk arbitrage and corporate governance. The Wyser-Pratte name has been synonymous with both risk arbitrage and corporate governance for as long as the terms have been used in the canyons that make up Wall Street.

Wyser-Pratte has been working on Wall Street for more than 30 years and is often called the dean of the arbitrage and corporate governance movement by friends and foes around the world. In the past few years, however, his efforts to champion shareholder rights and to change many aspects of corporate governance strategies have won him many headlines, as well as earning his investors superior returns during difficult and trying times in the markets around the globe.

"Our efforts to change the framework of corporate governance in the United States will destroy the 'just-say-no' defense that so many companies try to use when they are faced with a threat to their autonomy," he says. "It will end the abuses of *poison pill* and will force boards to think and act in the best interest of shareholders, something they often overlook."

poison pill

any of a number of legal defensive tactics written into a corporate charter to fend off the advances of an unwanted suitor.

"People are fed up with the way management has been using poison pills. Instead of using them as tools to protect the company and its shareholders, management has been using poison pills as tools for entrenchment," he continued.

The poison pill was invented in the 1980s to give management significant control over the success or failure of a hostile takeover bid. Poison pills give shareholders the right to purchase hundreds of millions of dollars worth of shares very cheaply, which in turn often scares the suitor off because of the significantly increased number of shares needed to gain control.

Wyser-Pratte believes that instead of benefiting the shareholder, the use of poison pills often harms them, because bidders aware of the pills' existence will not attempt a takeover. This keeps shareholders from realizing the maximum value of their investment and allows management to keep power. Therefore, he has designed the "chewable poison pill."

He says, "Our pill keeps the best aspects of the conventional poison pill but at the same time it does not allow management to entrench themselves. It forces management to act in the best interests of shareholders at all times."

The first example of the chewable poison pill's use came in late 1997, when Union Pacific Resources Inc. withdrew its unfriendly bid to take over Pennzoil Corp. Union Pacific had offered $84 a share for Pennzoil, but the oil company threw up a just-say-no defense. The unsolicited bid offered a $20-a-share premium and would have added $1 billion to the company's market capitalization. Once Union Pacific pulled out, however, Wyser-Pratte stepped in, figuring that there was no basis for management's turning the deal away. By July 30, 1998, Pennzoil stock was trading in the low $40 range. In late 1997, the stock was trading in the mid $60s.

Wyser-Pratte forced the company to act in the best interests of shareholders—he was one, since his fund owned over 1.5 percent of Pennzoil—by merging one of its units. It also has adopted a modified poison pill that gives shareholders a voice in future takeover offers. The chewable pill that Pennzoil adopted, based on Wyser-Pratte's efforts, says that if an unsolicited offer comes in at 35 percent over the average trading price, management must take it.

To make the board listen to his ideas, Wyser-Pratte launched a proxy fight, ran for a board seat, and filed a federal lawsuit to change a bylaw regarding board elections. Both sides in early 1998 reached a settlement that included Pennzoil's adding an outside director to its board and adopting a bylaw that gives shareholders the right to call a special meeting outside the annual meeting.

As part of the settlement, Wyser-Pratte dropped his lawsuit and his efforts to become a board member. Wyser-Pratte does not believe it will be the last time he will be able to get a company to adopt his chewable pill.

He has since moved on to fighting the poison pills and their protectors in general instead of in individual companies. As a Marine, he learned about fighting and more importantly about winning.

Wyser-Pratte believes that his effort to change corporate governance is doing what is right by the shareholders. This sentiment was not often echoed in the hedge fund community until recently and now is a flavor of the day for many fund managers.

"When management hides behind their poison pill, they undo whatever amount of corporate democracy exists and make a mockery out of corporate governance," he argues.

He became interested in corporate governance issues when he was running Prudential Bache's arbitrage group. In 1974 he owned preferred stock in the sugar company Great Western United, but when the time came to receive his dividends, he realized something was amiss. Sugar prices were surging, but the checks never arrived. Finally, he and a colleague decided to sue the company for the dividends they were owed. Within a matter of days of the filing of the suit, a check arrived from the company, and he realized that he could make money by becoming a shareholder activist.

Before 1974, he had been an arbitrageur. In its most simple definition, arbitrage is the buying of an article in one market and selling it in another. He learned the business of equity arbitrage from his father, who started the Wyser-Pratte firm in 1929 in Paris. It was subsequently merged into Bache & Co. and then into Prudential. In 1990, Wyser-Pratte resurrected the firm as a standalone entity—severing his ties with Prudential and operating the firm independently as his father had before him.

Wyser-Pratte usually works on three or four deals at a time, some in the United States and some in Europe.

"We try to focus on the best opportunities and work very hard at making them work for us instead of working on as many deals as possible," he says. "The way we determine what is worth doing is by looking at the amount of risk we have to take compared to the rate of return we expect from taking the risk. Something with a low return with a high risk is something we would avoid, while something with a high return with low risk is something we would be very interested in working on."

Another situation that Wyser-Pratte was involved with was Taittinger S.A., the French hotel and champagne conglomerate, of which he and his partners control approximately 13 percent of the stock.

"We keep accumulating the stock and telling management that they have got to do what is right for shareholders. We are drawing attention to the undervalued assets in the company," he says. "Over there, what we are doing is admired by the shareholder population, but the establishment hates our guts."

The fund's efforts to increase shareholder value in Taittinger S.A. were the subject of a front-page article in the *Wall Street Journal.*

Wyser-Pratte usually gets involved when a buyer walks away from a deal because the company has refused to accept the offer that is on the table. Once he gets involved, he works to make the deal happen. Although he does not talk to the suitor or have any kind of agreement with the company, his efforts are always focused on maximizing value for shareholders—which usually include him.

"In most cases when buyers walk away from a deal, they are expecting us to get involved, to run the company up a yardarm somewhere," he says. "Most suitors know that if we think the company is not acting in the best interest of the shareholder, we will turn our guns on them and make them maximize shareholder value."

There have been a number of times when Wyser-Pratte has heard of a situation and for whatever reason decided to get involved not by purchasing stock but strictly as an activist. Two cases of this were with the American International Group's attempt to buy American Bankers Insurance without letting others bid on it and Echlin Inc.'s attempt to get an anti-shareholder law passed in Connecticut. In both cases, his funds owned stock in the companies, but Wyser-Pratte felt that he needed to take action to force the companies to look out for their shareholders.

"When you see that you can actually get things done by having the force of conviction to actually do something, that makes it fun," he says.

In the early spring of 2010, Wyser-Pratte was mixing both arbitrage and corporate governance. He was working on a number of deals both in Europe and the United States and seemed to be having fun.

"The arb deals are in full swing," he said in his office overlooking Park Avenue. "There a lot of deals that are being announced, both friendly and hostile, and there is a lot to do."

One problem with his strategy is something he calls a liquidity mis-match. The deals that he works on specifically in the corporate governance or activist strategy often take years to come to a conclusion, and as such investors have to be locked up for some time before they not only can get their money out but also reap any benefits.

"I think the solution is to create a series of special purpose vehicles that are created specifically for a target, one company, one SPV," he said. "Once we get people who buy into the target, we will raise the money work the deal."

He believes that doing transactions this way through special purpose vehicles will allow him to be more successful at raising money, getting deals done, and, most importantly, solving the liquidity mismatch.

Prior to launching the firm, Wyser-Pratte managed money at Prudential Bache. His performance record includes all of the years for which he managed money both in and outside of Prudential.

His firm currently operates out of mid-town Manhattan in the heart of New York's new financial district. For the most part, he makes all investment decisions and works with colleagues to implement his strategies. Since the firm has been independent, Wyser-Pratte has completed many corporate governance deals, both in the United States and in Europe, and all have been successful. His investors are both high-net-worth individuals and pension funds.

Wyser-Pratte's efforts and interest in corporate governance have come from paying close attention to what goes on in Europe.

"Our experience operating overseas has taught us how to work around a lot of the issues we are faced with here in the United States," he says. "Overseas, they don't have this nonsense. The key idea over there is to protect shareholders, not to entrench management. Here, because of the American Bar Association, the whole thing is to perpetuate litigation around the poison pill, and all they are doing is wasting shareholder money."

Although he has taken the lead on the takeover of such U.S. companies as Willamette Timber by Weyerhaeuser Corporation, these days he's focusing on Europe. Why turn your sights on a hotbed of government-sanctioned cronyism and old? The market punishes companies for poor management, making firms like Vivarte of France, Vendex of the Netherlands, and IWKA of Germany underpriced and therefore lucrative targets. "Corporate managers who consistently destroy value in a free market are replaced by good managers," he said.

But he acknowledges that he's found the going tougher on the other side of the pond. If European establishment interests have rendered corporations ripe for takeover, they've also insisted on putting up a fight. "There's more resistance on the part of establishment in Europe," he said. "In France, you have the old families who control a lot through double-voting rights. In Germany, it's the Socialist party that controls all the organs of justice. The company we're going after in Germany, not a single person on the board owns any stock. Not a single person in management owns any stock. What's wrong with this picture?"

To proceed, Wyser-Pratte builds what he refers to with a wink as a "coalition of the willing," a group of shareholders capable of pressuring companies and even governments into bending. In the end, whether they know it or not, the boards are forced to act in the companies' best interests. Vivarte (the former Group André), for instance, began, after the takeover in 2002, to show its first profits in years. "It's not just that you're trying to make money for people. As people have said about us over the years, we're on the side of the angels. We're trying to benefit everybody." Indeed, he added, much of Europe still needs to be taught what it means to have an equity culture. For this, Wyser-Pratte directly blames the rule of Communism, which evaporated from the continent only 25 years ago.

He doesn't believe that European companies aren't out to make a profit. Rather, he argues that European families and governments see their companies as personal and national property, rather than as belonging to the shareholders who bought them on the open market. The issue is particularly galling when boards attempt to hide behind national law in direct opposition to the fundamental contract of the European Union (EU) drawn up in Rome in 1957.

What he'd most like, however, is for European corporations to embrace American-style business. "Stand up for yourself," he says. "Create the values."

Those who refuse, he envisions, will only stand in danger of ultimately bankrupting themselves. And as Taittinger, the great French champagne conglomerate that fought him in 2001 found out, even defeating Wyser-Pratte in the short term only opens the door to greater difficulties moving forward. When French courts blocked Wyser-Pratte's attempts at taking over Taittinger, he pulled out. But the company still found it necessary to restructure itself, incorporating much of what he had recommended.

Born in Vichy, France, in 1940, he moved to the United States with his family in 1947 and became a U.S. citizen in 1953. Wyser-Pratte graduated from New York University with an MBA. The Marine Corps discharged him as a captain in 1966. He learned arbitrage from his father, Eugene Wyser-Pratte, who practiced the classical arbitrage strategy of buying stocks in one market and selling them in another.

"I did not find his business interesting at all," Wyser-Pratte recalls. "He explained to me that the business was getting more interesting and more intellectually challenging, so I decided to give it a look."

In 1967, his father decided to merge the family firm into Bache & Co. to have access to a larger pool of capital. He stayed with the firm until retiring in January 1971.

Guy Wyser-Pratte took over the unit and eventually came to run all of Prudential Bache's arbitrage activities. The situation became contentious in the late 1980s and early 1990s when Prudential was reeling from its limited partnership problems. When he was told that the firm had no more capital to use for proprietary trading because the securities firm's parent, Prudential Insurance Company of America, had shut it off, he decided to leave in 1991.

"In 1992, I did a lot of road shows and all I could raise was $3 million," he remembers. "But since then we have grown to our current size, and I think we are doing very well. There is nothing quite like running your own show, and it is particularly helpful with all we do in corporate governance because we don't have to ask before we go after a company."

Asking proved to be a problem when he was working at Prudential Bache. Wyser-Pratte sued Houston Natural Gas because the board had turned down a bid and had prevented a subsequent bid from coming into the boardroom. He cleared the suit right to the top of Prudential after explaining that the firm's interests had been damaged. No one checked with the president, however, who happened to be in the office of the chairman of Houston, Natural Gas at the minute the news flashed on the tape saying "Pru-Bache Files Suit Against Houston Natural Gas."

"The chairman was about to sign a huge investment banking deal with Prudential, and needless to say it did not get signed," he says. "Eventually, the chairman of Houston Natural Gas was fired for his actions, and another firm emerged to take over the company."

Wyser-Pratte believes that his training in the Marine Corps is the most formative experience he has ever had and that it has played a significant part in his ability to succeed in business: "Being a Marine has helped me tremendously on Wall Street in building my career. It taught me how to size people up when I am in a situation where character is called on. You can judge pretty quickly who you can count on and who you can't when there is danger, and that skill is very important to being successful on Wall Street."

On average, Wyser-Pratte and his team are working on between five and 10 deals at a time. The reason Europe is such a fruitful marketplace for his work is because of the continent's lack of liquidity and the local control that exists at many companies.

"In Europe, only 65 percent of all shares in companies are one-share-equals-one-vote; that is an extraordinary anomaly, when compared to the United States," he said. "The companies are set up to protect the interest of the family and the local communities, and this lack of accountability creates the opportunity because things are undervalued."

It takes a lot of work and effort to see the deals/transaction through to the end, but seeing it through makes it worth it.

"I don't mind the work; I was born to struggle," he said jokingly. "The opportunities are there, and we are going to grab them."

Wyser-Pratte believes that as long as he keeps his discipline and does not go crazy in one situation, while going about his business methodically, he will continue to be successful.

"The key to being successful in this business is to continue to get better at what we are trying to do," he says. "We need to stay focused on strategies that we know will work and build our skills around those strategies."

Wyser-Pratte believes that there are more important things in life than just lining both his and his investors' pockets.

"I am not involved with philanthropy in my business; my job is to make a decent return for investors," he says. "However, all of us in life look for some moral dimension in what we do, and I am able to fulfill that in what I do for a living."

Bill Michaelcheck—Mariner Investment Group

On Wall Street, there are stock guys and bond guys.

The stock guys can name all 30 Dow Jones Industrial Average stocks and at what level they opened and closed. The bond guys hang on Ben Bernanke and the Federal Reserve board's every word and laugh when the popular press reminds their readers and viewers that yield moves in the opposite direction of price.

I am a bond guy. All of my formal Wall Street training was at a bond house, and for awhile it was the way I made the bulk of my living.

So naturally, when I saw Bill Michaelcheck on one of the cable news channels talking about the Treasury market and his hedge fund, I became interested in learning more about him and his operation. This was more than 10 years ago, and as I have developed to learn more and more about the equity markets, he has continued to evolve his firm to include equities as well.

Michaelcheck is a bond guy. Since the early 1970s, after earning an MBA at Harvard, he has been trading Treasuries. He spent the early part of his career at J. F. Eckstein and Co. and the World Bank before finding a home at Bear Stearns & Co. Inc., where he built the Wall Street powerhouse's bond department. Working alongside Wall Street legend Alan "Ace" Greenberg, Michaelcheck created a significant business at Bear Stearns and, as a partner in the private firm that eventually went public, was rewarded handsomely.

In 1992, Michaelcheck launched Mariner Investment Group, a traditional hedge fund, in order to have a safe vehicle to manage his money. At the time we met in the spring of 2010, the organization had around $11 billion in assets under management with more than 165 employees.

"Over the past few years, our organization has evolved into what I would call a professional manager," he says. "That means we manage money in-house and that we also allocate money to other fund managers."

fund of funds

an investment vehicle that invests in other hedge funds.

Mariner currently has a number of products that it uses to manage its partners' money. The firm offers a series of hedge funds with trade strategies ranging from low-risk U.S. Treasury arbitrage to many equity-based strategies. It also offers a *fund of funds* that is managed through allocations to both inside and outside money managers.

"Today, hedge funds have become mainstream," he said. "Hedge funds fall into two categories, those that can attract assets and become large growing concerns and those that can't and remain going concerns but never get to critical mass."

Michaelcheck believes his organization continues to be successful because the needs of investors as well as the landscape of the industry have changed dramatically in the past five years.

"It used to be that there was some worldly guy who was a senior partner at some firm, who had $10 million in hedge fund investments with five different friends," he says. "Now you have big family offices and institutions that are putting out hundreds of millions of dollars in $10 million and $20 million chunks and they don't want to spread it around to guys sitting in their garage in Greenwich smoking cigars. It scares them, because if the manager blows up, the guy loses his job."

"So we are fashioning ourselves as an asset management firm that does hedge funds both internally and externally," he continues. "We are not consultants—we are hands-on managers who have been on the Street and understand that past performance is *not* an indication of future performance."

Michaelcheck thinks he is setting an example because, unlike others who have tried to build similar types of businesses, he and his colleagues were traders and are traders. They are in the markets daily and have been around the markets for a very long time.

"We have created a better mousetrap both internally and externally," he asserts. "We are not trying to be a personality cult. We want the business to be a business and we don't want our income hinging on the health of one of us."

Mariner evolved into its current form after Michaelcheck realized that there was an opportunity to provide to others the service that he needed for his own wealth.

"We are something like a fund of funds and we are a hedge fund," he says. "We are basically something completely unique in the world in which we operate."

At its offices in midtown Manhattan, the company trades fixed-income securities employing various arbitrage strategies in the Treasury and corporate bond markets. The firm also trades technology stocks using stock-versus-warrant arbitrage strategies to capture profits through market movements.

Mariner currently has a number of products that it uses to manage its partners' money. It operates traditional hedge funds—primarily in the credit and fixed-income markets—that offer investors low risk with steady moderate return streams and a fund of funds. The fund of funds is invested in managers outside of the firm while all of its hedge funds are managed by internal managers.

"We have built a platform for institutional investors," said Michaelcheck. "By working with both proprietary managers and external managers we are able to deliver consistent returns to our clients."

The firm's main office is in a nondescript office complex in Harrison, New York, about a 30-minute ride north of New York City. The idea is to put the bulk of its people under one roof in order to better serve the firm's investors and customers.

"It makes sense to move everybody to one location; it will make us more efficient," he said.

"We primarily run a low-risk hedge fund that takes advantage of price discrepancies in various fixed-income markets," he says. "We are not in this to get our adrenaline up; we are in this to make reasonable returns as risk-free as we possibly can. By putting on lots of small trades that allow us to pick up a few basis points here and there, we are able to accomplish this goal."

The money the firm farms out goes to managers whose styles range from high-yield arbitrage and takeover arbitrage to other arbitrage strategies. The difference between what the firm does itself and what it farms out is that the outside managers use "a little higher octane" than do the in-house handlers.

"Having come from the bond world, I do not have much faith in directional equity trading. While things appear to be easy right now, I have not found them to be easy and don't believe in it," he says. "I want to be able to understand what happens and what I think should happen, and do not want to rely on the Dow Jones Industrial Average. I don't need to hit home runs. I am happy employing strategies that have very little risk but allow me to pick up lots of nickels and dimes instead of occasionally picking up dollars."

Michaelcheck finds potential managers to invest with through word of mouth.

"People seem to know what we are doing and give us a call and tell us to check out this person or that person, and we look and see if what they are doing fits our investment criteria," he says. "We don't care about how a fund ranks or rates on the various industry databases because it is not how we operate. We know a lot of people who know a lot of people who give us ideas."

The firm looks for fund managers who are employing arbitrage and other market-neutral strategies, as well as those using event-driven business strategies, like takeovers, divestitures, spin-offs, and bankruptcies, things that the managers can thoroughly understand and wrap their heads around. Once Michaelcheck determines which funds to invest in, he performs stress tests on the portfolio and tries to come up with a balanced portfolio of funds that can produce solid returns over various market conditions.

Michaelcheck believes that it is virtually impossible to pick stocks. If you look at all the mutual funds of the world and all their portfolio managers, he believes very few know what they are doing.

"There are always a few exceptions but statistically speaking you are more likely to find diamonds in a mound of coal," he says. "Therefore, if no one can pick stocks, then no one can pick long and short stocks, and most hedge funds are throwing darts at a board."

"Everyone's stockbroker, every mutual fund manager, and almost every hedge fund manager claims to be the one person in the world who can pick stocks, and 99 percent of them cannot," he continues. "Being a hedge fund manager focused solely on stocks is a great marketing tool that is good for business, but for the most part the investors are getting the shaft."

Michaelcheck says that most of the hedge funds in today's marketplace do not add value to investors, and he believes that this is becoming more and more evident when the market moves sideways.

"If you look at the risk-adjusted returns of many hedge funds compared to those of the S&P or Treasuries, you find that very few categories of hedge funds have a positive alpha," he points out. "And most are just chugging along with the market. Chugging along with the market is not worth 1 percent plus 20," he says, alluding to hedge funds' usual management fees. "People are better off in index funds."

He continues, "Most of the hedge funds today earn money, good money, but they have a tremendous amount of volatility, and as such the investor would be better off leveraging up the S&P. But, if you look at what we or others like us do, we have volatility that is less than the five-year Treasury and are able to sustain reasonable growth no matter what the market situation."

"These are brilliant investment managers, but with all the ups and downs, the only guys making money are the hedge fund guys, because they are able to get 1 percent of total assets," he says. "Meanwhile, we are left waiting for them to do something for us."

"Stock hedge funds are going to be the first to fall out of favor because managers will not be able to put up 20 percent returns without taking enormous amounts of risk," he continues. "Customers will pull money like they did in 1968, and the industry will take a number of steps backward."

Regardless of this situation, Michaelcheck believes that by employing hedging strategies and looking at risk-adjusted returns, he will be able to provide very good returns with very little risk.

"We do not move our money around," he says. "One of the good things about our position is that we have a steady stream of good ideas."

Michaelcheck got the idea of offering a fund of funds when a number of people he called asked him what he was doing with his own money.

"I was interested in taking a somewhat more aggressive amount of risk with some of my personal money, so I started a fund of funds for that, and then slowly people heard about it and asked if they could get in," he says. "I do not market it. It is basically people saying, 'What are you doing with your money?' and one thing leads to another."

Beside the structure of his organization, also setting Michaelcheck apart from other hedge fund managers is that the firm does not always go for the jugular when it moves in and out of the market.

"Our trading strategy is not very glamorous: Our philosophy is to stay rich and not get richer," he says. "We like to sleep at night and enjoy other obligations. When we get nervous, we realize that we are not doing what we set out to do and quickly get back on track."

Nancy Havens—Havens Advisors LLC

Clearly Wall Street is a place where the old boys' network is very much alive and kicking. No matter how far we have come, it is still very hard for women to achieve the same prominence as men. Many women try and, for the sole reason of their gender, fail.

One woman who has managed to succeed is Nancy Havens.

The fifty-something hedge fund manager, who has an MBA from Harvard and an undergraduate degree from Cornell, broke through the Wall Street boys' club in a very big way. Besides being the first woman elected to the Bear Stearns & Co. Inc. board of directors, she is also considered by some to be the first woman investment banker ever to hit the Street. Now she is one of a handful of successful women hedge fund managers.

In 1995, she left the comfort of Bear, Stearns & Co. Inc.,—where she managed more than 100 people, had responsibility for a trading account in excess of half a billion dollars, and was one of the company's 15-highest-paid employees—to start a hedge fund.

Her fund, Havens Partners, which had just over $250 million under management in the winter of 2005, specializes in risk arbitrage and distressed debt. With a team of eleven, Havens trades the debt and equity markets looking for unique opportunities that she can exploit for a profit.

Through the end of 2009, Havens Partners, the firm's domestic fund, was up 9.87 percent. A thousand dollars invested with the fund at inception in January 1996 would have been worth just over $3,400 at year-end 2009. Over the years Havens has tried to build a team that complements each other, works well together, and most importantly, gets along with each other. "When you are working in a relatively small space, it is important that everyone gets along and can work well together," she said. "It is really a team effort."

Over the past few years, the firm has continued to jockey the line between merger arbitrage, distressed, and high yield. Havens and her team are constantly looking for opportunities to invest across these areas of the investment world.

"Our team is strong, and we are able to take advantage of situations that others miss because we are so nimble and focused," she said.

Havens decided to get out of Bear Stearns because she felt she had risen as high up in the corporation as she could.

"I left Bear Stearns because I had gotten to a very narrow part of the pyramid, and I knew that as a female I would not get any higher," she says. "I had got to where I got because I made money and I never had a losing year while I worked at the firm. When I got on the board, I suddenly found myself in a situation where it did not matter if you made money and it became 100 percent political, and I like making money more than playing politics."

Havens, who is married and the mother of two children, believes that it would have taken an enormous amount of work and probably a change in her personality to move higher at Bear Stearns, and she was not willing to do it. So she decided to leave and set up her own fund.

"I don't get my jollies from playing politics. I get my jollies from making money, and I realized that I should get myself into a situation where I could be happy full time," she says. "I enjoyed working within my own department and performing the research to get the job done but I did not enjoy the political aspects of the job."

Now Havens works for herself and her partners to make money. Although she still has to deal with political/office issues like who the health-care coordinator or the network administrator is, it's all for her own benefit. One thing that has taken getting used to is that when there is an equipment problem she can't pick up the phone and see immediate results.

"When I was at Bear, if my machine went down or something stopped working, I could call the help desk and they knew because of my title and position that they had to help me right away," she says. "Now there is no one to call, and when we finally do get in touch with something we are always at the bottom of the list. It takes a lot of getting used to, but over time I am sure it will be well worth it."

Her initial interest in risk arbitrage came after a stint as an equity analyst covering the computer industry.

"I was looking for something that would keep me interested," she says. "I had been an investment banker and covered stocks and got bored. Arbitrage was very interesting to me at the time, and it has become something I love."

Today the fund specializes in risk arbitrage and distressed debt, but because of market conditions it has very minimal positions in distressed debt and has a focus on high-yield bonds.

"For the past year, distressed debt has been a pretty untenable place to be. Default rates have been at an all-time low, and there were a lot of people who raised a lot of money when defaults were at an all-time high They were all chasing a tiny bit of merchandise, and the risk-reward was bad," she says.

Havens believes in understanding every angle before getting into a trade and executing an order.

"When I don't know a market very well but it has totally fallen on its side, I will go in and buy the highest-quality instrument I can find and take the first 20 points out and let someone else have the next 30," she says. "That is the game I like. I am truly a vulture, and I like it very much."

Havens has spent a significant amount of time doing garden-variety risk arbitrage. Her definition of that is going long on the acquired company and shorting the requisite amount of the acquirer if it is a stock-for-stock deal. If it is a cash deal, she buys at the spread and works to protect herself should the deal fall through.

"In this type of market, it is very important to have the highest-quality deals you can find," she says. "If I think there is an enormous amount of downside I will buy puts to give up part of my upside to protect my downside. If the downside looks like a cliff, you don't want to be looking over the cliff without anything to hold onto."

The spreads are very narrow right now. In 2010, the time was ripe for deals: The Dow was down for the first few weeks of the year, the companies had lots of cash, and, more importantly, they had lots of stock.

And although the firm focuses most of its attention on the United States, it does sometimes look for opportunities in Europe and even Asia that may make sense to get into. "There has been a lot going on over in Europe," she said. "The difficulty in accessing these markets is information; You are in the wrong time zone, far away, and you don't necessarily speak the language."

As the market continues to move along, the deal flow is sure to increase and when it does, Havens is going to be ready.

"There will be lots of opportunities once the market shakes out," she predicts. "A lot of the distressed guys have been hit pretty bad because they have held on to their positions, and now the competition in distressed is a whole lot less than it used to be."

To get information on deals, Havens uses a combination of internal analysis and standard Wall Street research. Having worked closely with the Street for so long, she has established a network of sources of information.

"We like to get information from people who know things, not just people who are repeating things they have heard from someone they don't really know," she says. "Whenever it is possible, I like to get in touch with people who really know what is going on so that I can make the best decision. Whatever is the problem with the deal or the area most likely to cause concern, I will try to figure out who I know who might have some insight on it."

When she started out, Havens found that she was too busy just getting the business going.

"It was amazing to me how hard it was to start this business and how many stupid details there are that need to be covered in order to get things up and running," she says.

"We were last on the list for things to get done for many of the companies we work with, and that was a big change for me coming from Bear, where people knew that if I had a problem it needed to be fixed immediately and properly the first time," she says. "When you are not a member of the firm any longer, everyone else comes before you."

In the past year or so she has been able to break away from those tasks and do what she likes to do: research.

"I like doing the research and finding deals," she says. "It is important to understand what is going on in a particular situation in order to make sure you get the most out of it."

She also likes sticking to what she knows and understands.

"In order to be a good arbitrageur, you have to like to analyze a lot. It is like a game," she says. "It is about understanding the personalities and why the deal makes sense from a business standpoint as well as understanding what snakes are in the road between here and consummation. It is really a lot of fun because you are always learning something new and on the cusp of new technology."

Although she is constantly learning about new industries and companies, she does not believe in changing her strategy just to put up performance numbers. She thinks that when things start moving against her the best thing to do is to get out and wait for the market to turn.

"We will not have a position in our portfolio that is greater than six percent of our assets under management," she says. "I am not interested in taking unnecessary risks just to put up strong numbers. It is better to sit things out and wait for situations you understand than to go looking for things that you really don't understand and hope work out."

Havens sees the most important part of her business as understanding how to manage risk and how to hedge to protect capital.

"Many people don't have any idea how to hedge or manage risk and therefore get into trouble," she says. "In order to be successful, you need to understand the instruments and how they trade, because if you don't, one deal can wipe out your whole business—especially if you are leveraged 11 to 1."

The main focus for her fund is to show strong results so she can continue to build the business.

"The best thing for us to do is to be ready for any direction in which the market would go," she says. "I think that we are on the brink of a real disaster, one in which the world goes into a major recession and takes us with them. The market could swing 400 points in either direction, and we need to make sure we are prepared when and if that happens."

The fund ended up with a strong fourth quarter finishing 2009 at over six percent. Havens said she was able to take advantage of what she called "a mediocre market" that allowed her to "load up" on lots of bargains and ride the wave as the market recovered.

One of the rules she lives by is something that a good friend who is a hedge fund manager told her when she was starting the fund: "Never bet the business on one trade."

Steve Cohen—SAC Capital

Outside of Wall Street, nobody seems to know who Steve Cohen is. Although he has been the subject of a handful of articles, he is rarely quoted directly. He has been dubbed "The Most Powerful Trader on Wall Street You've Never Heard Of" by *BusinessWeek* and called the best stock trader around.

Yet in the hedge fund world he is a giant. His company, SAC Capital, was managing just north of $8.6 billion in assets with more than 1,882 investment holdings, according to a 13F filing with the SEC made at the end of 2004. This is up considerably from when he was profiled in the first edition of this book in 2000. At that time, the firm had under $1 billion in assets under management. On any given day the firm trades nearly 20 million shares, equaling nearly three percent of the daily volume on the New York Stock Exchange and nearly one percent of the volume on NASDAQ. It is estimated that the firm generates nearly $150 million in commissions per year to Wall Street brokers, making it a very important account.

Cohen is probably one of the best-known unknown hedge fund managers in the world. He started his business in 1992 after spending a number of years trading stocks and options at Gruntal & Co. Since then he has built a business that has never had a down year and has grown to be one of the hedge fund world's most sought-after investments. Although Cohen was trained by experience while working at Gruntal & Co., his formal trading education came at a very early age.

"I am a tape reader," he says. "I learned how to trade stocks by going into my local brokerage firm office when I was 13 and watching the tape. From there, I was able to determine what was going on, how things were trading, and most importantly how to see opportunities from numbers moving across the screen."

Today his fund organization consists of more than watching the tape. SAC Capital employs over 200 people, who range from traders and analysts to back-office support and clerical people. The fund, headquartered in Stamford, Connecticut, has an office in New York City.

Since inception, the fund has put up significant numbers—on average 40 percent per year. As Marcia Vickers said in her *BusinessWeek* article, his ability is "almost like turning water into vintage Bordeaux." Cohen and his partners are some of the largest investors in the fund. Their investment consists of more then 60 percent of the firm's assets under management. When it comes to performance, Cohen and his traders are on the ball.

Cohen still believes that knowledge of situations and ideas is the key to success.

"This is an information business and the only way to be successful is to pay attention to what is going on and find situations that make sense," he says.

"One of the reasons we do as well as we do is because we cover most of the sectors in the S&P and also have unique trading backgrounds."

"We do not get married to positions. If things are not working the way that we had hoped that they would, we get out," he continues. "We don't just sit there and let things happen; we are very active and always making trades according to what is going on in the market."

As SAC has increased its assets under management it has also been constantly evolving its trading strategies, styles, and techniques.

"The more capital you have to move around, the less you can move around as quickly, so consequently you have to develop a system that has a model that allows you to hold on to stocks even if the reasons why you went into the stocks have changed or your time frame has changed," says Cohen. "It is not a question of liquidity, because the markets are fairly liquid, and we are in a lot of the big names. But the reality is, as we have gotten bigger, we need to have more reasons as to why we own something."

Cohen says that prior to opening SAC, when he was trading significantly smaller amounts of capital, he was able to buy 50,000 shares of IBM simply because he thought the market was going up. He based his decision solely on the tape and what he saw on the screen.

"I would make the decision to buy on the simple fact that I thought it was going up and I liked the way it looked without any fundamental reason as to why I liked IBM," he says. "Now we might buy IBM for a number of reasons. It might be that the computer sector is strong or that the analysts have expectations that things are going well. We now use different catalysts to make decisions as to whether we want to own something or sell something."

Cohen believes that one of the factors that has made his job harder is the explosive growth in the number of individual investors trading stocks—in particular those trading on the Internet. He believes that for the most part many of the investors trading electronically are momentum investors: When they see something go up, they buy it but don't have any real understanding of what is going on or why a stock's price is moving.

"My guess is that it is almost like a casino," he says. "The moves in stocks are larger and quicker than ever before, and it seems like there is a bandwagon effect. When something is moving, everyone wants to get on."

This has caused Cohen to adapt his trading style and pay closer attention to the price movements.

"If there is a piece of news out that I am going to discount because I don't think it is a big deal, normally I would go in and short the stock. But now I have to wait a little bit because things could get really crazy because there are so many other people involved in the game now," he says. "It is really unbelievable, and I am going to make a fortune off of it."

An example of how Cohen has adapted his trading style and the changes in the game to his advantage is with a trade in USA Networks, Inc., and its then newly listed subsidiary, Ticketmaster Online—City Search, Inc. In the last days before the initial public offering (IPO) of Ticketmaster, USA Networks stock started moving up and Cohen decided to short the issue. His experience told him that in most cases when a parent spins out a subsidiary, the parent's price gets a big run-up, and then when the IPO hits—boom!—the parent falls like a rock.

Although Cohen would not say at what price he went short or at what price he covered, prior to the IPO the stock traded as high as $32 a share and then fell to $28. His short position consisted of over half a million shares.

"This is an example of how the phenomena of individual investors and Internet jockeys are causing the prices to move dramatically," he says. "USA Networks was discounted 12 times and the price still went higher because there is a lot of nonsense in the market right now. If the rules of the game had not been changed, this stock would never have gotten to be higher than $31 or $32."

"Nothing stays the same in this business," he continues. "You have to constantly adapt and evolve and learn what the new game is and then play accordingly."

SAC divides its capital into styles and sector portfolios run by various traders and fund managers. These styles surround a core trading strategy that Cohen runs with eight traders. He believes that having traders trade in groups allows the funds to be more profitable.

"I want people to be less worried about individual P&Ls [profits and losses] and more tuned into how the group is performing on the whole," he says. "For instance, if a guy has a bad day and is down a million bucks, the next day he is going to come in and not want to play the game. However, if the group account is up two million, he is going to come in the next day and still be in the game and will be trading. Maybe he had a bad day and did not score any points, but maybe he had a few assists. We are trying a group approach, which over time will allow us to continue to perform extremely well."

Unlike other funds that charge fees of one percent plus 20 percent of profits, SAC has various fees based on the strategy or style the investor chooses. In some cases the fund charges as much as 50 percent of the profits without a management fee, while other styles and strategies charge the standard fees of one percent plus 20 percent of profits.

Cohen believes fees are justified by performance. He believes his funds have benefited from the carnage that laid waste to the industry.

"We benefit from volatility because we are opportunistic, and, when the markets get a little more volatile, there are more opportunities to trade," he says.

While Cohen is constantly changing his trading strategies to adapt to market forces, he is also changing the structure of his company.

"I can see running as many as 10 different funds in the next few years," he says. "We want to be able to offer different strategies to meet the various needs of investors. Some people may want risk arbitrage while others want to invest in a specific sector. We are essentially going to create an organization that caters to whomever is interested in investing with us. I would call us a group of hedge funds under a single hedge fund roof."

Cohen, who graduated from the University of Pennsylvania in 1977, got started on Wall Street in 1978 in Gruntal & Co.'s option arbitrage department after a friend of his brother's best friend got him the job.

"We basically would buy stock and hedge it with puts and calls," he says. "Back then it was a license to print money—everything was out of whack and it was really easy."

After a while, Cohen decided that hedging did not always make sense; he began to start holding on to positions and became a directional trader. When he first started trading at Gruntal, he never spoke with anyone or used research reports; he made all his decisions based on what he saw on the screen.

"In the old days you could actually watch the tape and see what was going on," he says. "Now the tape moves too fast and there are more factors involved in trading and price movements."

Today, he is covered by all the major brokerages and is swamped with research reports and analyst recommendations. Still, he very rarely speaks with analysts or brokers and instead relies on his staff to handle the calls and countless pages of information.

"What we need to do is differentiate who is good and who is not and how to discount the investment banking aspect of the information that they are providing to us," he says. "When you get to know analysts over time, as the relationship grows, they will tell you things that can help you make a good decision."

Cohen hires both seasoned and unseasoned Wall Streeters to work at SAC. Lately, he has been hiring fund managers who could not make it on their own but who seem to thrive in the right environment—his.

"There are a lot of guys who try to run their own fund but have a hard time growing the business into something meaningful and end up nowhere," he observes. "Many of them realize that they would be much better suited in an organization where a lot of the stuff that they normally have to do is already taken care of."

"We have a few guys in our shop who were okay on their own, really nothing great, but who have just exploded since they have started working with us," he continues. "My guess is that there will be a shakeout in the industry when guys are not making any money, and I bet we will see a lot of guys who want to work with us."

Cohen is not sure how big he wants his fund operation to grow.

"I don't want to get big and put myself under a lot of pressure, but I would like to get big if it was managed the right way," he says. "In order to do that we would bring in talent and set up new funds, which would allow me to mitigate the risk and concentrate on what I know how to do without having to worry about how others are going to affect my performance."

As Cohen evolves his operation he adapts to the changes that affect all of Wall Street. One of the things that has really changed since he started in the business is the reliance on technology.

"It used to be you came in in the morning and you left at 4:30 and then you come in the next morning and you trade again," he says. "Now because of all the information that is out there, it has really become a 24-hour-a-day job. This job keeps going and going and going."

He says he isn't sure whether the change is good or bad but that the standard answer is that the job has become more interesting. The downside, of course, is that traders now have to sit in front of a computer all day, and trading hours never end.

"This can be an all-consuming job, but it is fun. Every day there is something new," he says. "It is a game. It's like playing a sport every day."

Chapter 4

Hedge Fund Investing

When it comes down to it, there is no science to picking hedge funds or any investment, for that matter. For however many investors there are in hedge funds, there are at least as many different reasons why they picked that particular fund and actually gave the manager money to manage.

This chapter explains how various investors and consultants choose which hedge funds to invest in and why. Just as there are many different investment strategies managers employ to post returns, there are equally diverse ways to choose a hedge fund in which to invest one's hard-earned assets. Hopefully, by reading this chapter you will gain a better understanding of how people choose managers, what to look for in a manager, and what to avoid. The key to any successful investment decision is performing complete and thorough due diligence. Due diligence is not easy; it is a difficult task that takes time, patience, and experience. Remember: Just because someone calls themselves a hedge fund manager, has an office, and some documents, does not make it so. You need to get information and process it thoroughly before you commit to investing with a manager or firm. Take time and do your homework—the result will be worth it; trust me.

Prior to the credit crisis and again occurring in 2010, some investors believed that a manager was doing them a favor by accepting their money or taking their assets into their fund. This is nonsense. It's ridiculous and just plain silly. It is as silly as those agents or feeders who run around the world saying that they have access to managers that others don't and for that they should be paid a fee for providing entry into these funds. Don't do it. You will get burned. It is not worth it. If you really want a manager that is closed or is only accessible through an agent or feeder try going direct or finding an alternative.

If you think it is okay to invest this way, then stop investing now. You are going to get crushed. Similarly, if as a potential investor, a manager seems to be doing you a favor by letting you invest with him or her, well, again, take your money and move on. Madoff stole billions of dollars by acting this way—enough said.

There are many inexperienced investors who believe that hedge fund investors simply throw darts at a list of potential funds in order to find funds worthy of their assets or simply invest with friends or friends of friends. Unfortunately, they would be correct in this assumption; there are all types of ways of doing investment research, the least of which is simply looking at a list of funds that performed well during a given period and choosing one or two based on this information—thus dart throwing. What works for some may not work for others and vice versa. I don't recommend dart throwing; I recommend due diligence and lots of it. The best investor is an informed investor, someone who understands the strategy and understands how the manager implements it on a day to day basis. It takes time, it takes work, and it is not easy but again, it is your money, so do the right thing by it.

There is no one right way to invest or choose managers. And everybody's process is proprietary. People make their decisions, based on experience, knowledge, understanding, and gut. One thing is for sure about the process: as Peter Lynch, the famed Fidelity Investments mutual fund manager, said many years ago, "People spend more money picking out the color of their refrigerator than they do on picking stocks."

Lynch was talking about individual investors who do not have the wherewithal to perform due diligence on their investments and work off tips to invest, rather than doing the research. The statement applies to sophisticated and unsophisticated investors alike. How many times has someone passed you a tip? More importantly, how many times have you acted upon it and been burned?

When the truth about Madoff came out in December of 2008, many investors wailed with anger and looked to point a finger at somebody or something for not exposing him as a fraud sooner. These investors were angry at being taken by this now-legendary con-man and wanted justice or at least wanted someone to blame for their misfortune and to cover their losses. The reality is they have no one to blame but themselves. Call it greed, call it fear, call it status, or even call it naivety; these people wanted to call it anything but what it was—their own fault. Madoff existed because the market allowed him to, maybe there were signs that were ignored; maybe there were doubts being raised. But just as little kids believe that there really is a Santa Claus, investors, the Street, and even the Securities and Exchange Commission wanted to believe in Madoff. He is a master manipulator who played up the right things, played down the right things, and, most importantly, preyed upon his victims with grace, flair, and no regard for anything but satisfying his need to steal and rob from those who trusted him most.

The blame game is the latest and greatest tool used by society, not just in the wake of Madoff or the credit crisis, but for everything that goes wrong or not according to plan. Many people no longer want to take responsibility for their own actions or misfortunes. People are always looking for someone else to blame for the errors of their ways. A lot of this attitude comes from the people in Washington who have adopted a pass-the-buck mentality rather than the one Harry Truman made famous during his presidency. Taking responsibility for one's investments should be something everyone does regardless of how much money they have in their wallet. It all starts with due diligence.

One of the problems with investing in hedge funds is the lack of standardized information available about the industry, the funds, and the people who manage the portfolios. Unlike fixed income and equity investing where the data is clear, concise, and consistent, the same cannot be said for hedge fund manager information. There are many databases, consultants, and tools available that provide information about hedge funds for potential investors. However, because the data is not standardized, the due diligence process is difficult and all that harder to complete. The lack of standardized information and misinformation published in the media makes getting the answers often a difficult and arduous task. As I have said before, the popular press very rarely gets the story right about hedge funds. The problems with the media coverage does not rest solely in the hands of the press; some of this blame goes to the hedge funds themselves for not communicating properly and getting their messages out.

The press writes about two or three different individuals and assumes that they represent the entire industry. The press seems to focus on master-of-the-universe activities and the whole concept of shadowy figures moving markets. The recent arrest and indictment of a number of hedge fund folks for insider trading has not helped, however, this practice has been going on for years. Smart and thorough hedge fund investors understand that not all hedge funds are run by Steve Cohen, John Paulson, or George Soros even if the popular press does not, and, more importantly, that not all hedge funds are engaged in illegal activities to generate returns.

In order to get information, perform due diligence, and construct portfolios, both retail and institutional investors look to hedge fund consultants, investment advisers, and other professionals to help them make investment decisions. However even with professional advice and guidance, investors still make mistakes and choose the wrong funds.

One thing that seems to come into play is greed. Some investors look to hedge funds to satisfy their greed and to chase returns. And one thing that comes with chasing returns is hot money.

"A lot of people who invest in funds are doing so with hot money," says Steve Cohen. "These are people who put money with fund PDQ because it was up X percent last year and they believe it will do it again. However, as soon as the year-end comes and the fund does not meet expectations, boom, they pull their money and look to the next guy who is having or has had a good run."

Cohen says he believes most of the investors do not know why they get into specific funds. He feels that some of those who are not chasing hot managers are investing to feed egos or to keep up with the Joneses.

"People do very strange things when they invest," he says. "For the most part there is no rhyme or reason to their actions; they do it just to do it."

Cohen's sentiments are echoed by many of the consultants and analysts who help people choose fund managers and strategies. These consultants are investment advisers who specialize in the hedge fund world and for a fee will provide the investor access to their knowledge of the industry and its managers. As there are all types of investors, there are all types of advisers. Some work in conjunction with brokerage firms and hedge funds, acting as marketing agents for specific managers, while others work solely on behalf of the client and are paid a fee for their advice. For the most part, those who offer hedge fund consultant services are on the up-and-up. However as the industry has continued to grow and become more and more mainstream in the last few years, there have been many additions to the consulting industry. Be careful; there are many undesirable people out there who market themselves as experts, who claim objectivity, who frankly are going to steal from you. Beware of those who promise services that will lead to returns that are too good to be true.

Some of the most active hedge fund consultants are quoted in the popular press and interviewed on CNBC quite frequently. They are seen as able to provide an unadulterated view of the industry and of specific managers. However, there are just as many who have no scruples, double dip, take advantage of investors' naivety, and are completely unethical in the way they operate their businesses.

It is just as important to perform due diligence on the consultant as it is on the funds in which you invest your money. Do the work; it will be worth it.

The Role of an Investment Adviser

As Wall Street has continued to make its way to mainstream, a series of investment advisers has built successful businesses focusing solely on providing advice and guidance to individuals and institutions looking to invest in hedge funds.

These firms work with individuals, family offices, and institutions helping them with asset allocation, manager selection, and running their investment programs. These types of firms work solely for the client or investor. They are paid a fee on the asset that they advise on and, in turn—in theory—are working always in the best interest of their clients. There are some firms who work both sides of the trade—they advise clients and get a fee from managers for recommending funds to clients. The good ones should be conflict-free. It is important that during the due diligence process questions are asked and answered about potential or real conflicts.

Investment advisers should provide customized services to their clients and, for the most part, look to deliver a high level of service for the fees that they charge. There are a lot of people who offer these types of services, so investors can afford to be choosy. Most firms act as investment staff for hire.

Understanding the advisor's methodology is important. Clients should explain their risk tolerance, liquidity needs, and long-term and short-term goals for the assets. Advisors should create a strategy that meets or exceeds the goals and meets any specific investment criteria. The process for choosing or allocating assets to hedge fund managers is no different than that of other investments that are considered long-term in nature. Investors need to ask questions, get answers, and get involved in how their money is managed. The process should be completed by both parties. Advice should be given and reviewed and decisions should be made only after all the material is reviewed.

During the last few years, the press has been quick to report that turmoil had taken over the hedge fund industry as returns were bad and investors liquidated what if any of their assets were left in the hedge fund industry. However, since 2010 began, asset flows have started again and investors have once again started putting money back into hedge funds. Many are doing more due diligence and getting more involved in the allocation process. This is good, and it should continue. However, investors need not forget that they are responsible for their money and, therefore, need to ask questions and get answers that make sense before an allocation is made to a fund or strategy. Advisors who provide good solid service are an instrumental part of this process and should be used in an effort to avoid mistakes and errors when allocating assets.

An Institutional Investor

For the most part, when one reads or hears about hedge fund investors, people think of rich individuals and wealthy families. Although these groups are very active in investing in hedge funds, institutional investors are by far the largest and most important users of such vehicles.

These pension funds, insurance companies, banks, brokerages, and national and multinational corporations represent hundreds of billions of dollars invested in everything from plain-vanilla stocks and bonds to exotic derivatives and hedge funds.

Most of the investors operate in strict secrecy. An unwritten rule forbids these investors and the funds from disclosing who does and does not invest with specific funds.

"You will never get a fund to give up the name of an institutional investor because they represent too big an amount of investment dollars," says an industry observer.

To understand the process that institutional investors use to determine where and how much they will invest, one needs to get to the investment decision maker.

Unfortunately, most if not all institutional investors hesitate to explain their allocation and investment strategies on the record. One institutional investor who is very active in hedge funds agreed to be interviewed, but only if no names were used.

The pension fund is charged with managing $45 billion. At the end of 2009, it had allocated 20 percent of its assets to hedge funds—up from 15 percent in 2004. When we spoke in January, it was invested in 16 hedge funds, all of which manage their money internally and use long/short market-neutral strategies.

The institution's philosophy is to pursue investments at the forefront of the pension investment process to be able to make additional returns. It is willing to do things that other pension funds are not.

"If the others are not making the investment for a pure risk issue," says one of the pension fund's managing directors, "and if we think that is one of the primary reasons for not making the investment, we believe it will create extra returns for our portfolio."

The pension fund tries to control risk very tightly where its managers believe risk can become an issue. So, for example, it exercises very tight controls over its fixed-income program and moderate controls over its U.S. equity program.

"Exercising control allows us more latitude to take more risk with a long/short program or higher-returning market-neutral and absolute-return strategies," explains one of the pension fund's managing directors.

"We have chosen the funds we are with because we believe that fundamentally they have unique insight and investment capacity and capability coupled with excellent risk controls," the managing director says. "Those three attributes are consistent throughout our entire investment program, and we believe by applying them to hedge funds—which turns the dial up a little bit—we will be able to attain significant returns without adding significant risk."

The institution believes that investing in long/short strategies provides for a more efficient use of its capital. As such it plans on moving money from long-only managers who focus on matching the indexes to long/short managers who focus on individual stock selection.

"By changing our strategies we believe we are going to be able to leverage our managers' ability to add value and hopefully increase returns at the same time," the managing director says.

The pension fund allocates money by looking at the track record and diversification the hedge fund managers bring to the program. If they pass the review, the fund allocates between $50 million and $100 million to them.

"We will add managers as we add assets," the managing director says. "But we also realize that managers have a life span and some of our managers are decaying, so the trick for us is to determine when a manager has reached the top and then move on to another fund. Hopefully, we can get out of the fund before it hits bottom. The real test to the program is to not hold on to one fund too long."

The pension fund plans to drop one of its hedge funds in the next year and plans to add six additional hedge funds to its portfolio.

The pension fund limits its stake in a particular fund to 20 percent of its total assets. It believes that the best way to add value to its portfolio is to find young managers and grow with them.

"We are a big fund and it does not make sense for us to screw around with a $10-million chunk," the managing director says. "We are looking for a manager who can grow into becoming a $2 billion fund, and, if this is the case, we may start with a $50 million position and grow with the fund to the point of allocating it $200 million to $300 million."

The pension fund doesn't use consultants to help pick hedge funds but its executives believe that, as it expands, they may do so. They plan, for example, to hire a fund of funds manager to gain access to some hedge funds that it otherwise would not be able to invest in.

due diligence

questions by investors to the manager regarding investment style and strategy as well as the manager's background and track record.

"When it comes to investing in hedge funds, people are very conscious and cognizant of making sure *due diligence* is performed and the right choices are made," the managing director says. "We want to be very thorough and dig under the surface of the funds to make sure that we do not make a mistake, and we realize that we cannot do it on our own."

"The advantage of hiring a fund of funds manager is that you can get into some funds where there is a smaller slice available—say a $10 million or $15 million piece," he continues. "Also, we can insulate ourselves from the risk perspective and we can blame them if things do not go well."

The pension fund will look for fund of funds managers the same way it looks for individual fund or money managers. It will choose a fund of funds that has a competitive edge, can be trusted, employs good risk control, and can share due diligence as well bring good funds to its portfolio.

"It is not simply a risk-versus-return issue with a fund of funds," the managing director says. "We are looking for a partner that can help us expand our use of hedge funds."

The managing director believes that many institutional investors make investment decisions based on historical attributes and the manager's reputation rather than looking ahead at how the manager could be expected to perform. While he believes this is a mistake for anyone, it can be a disaster with long/short hedge funds because it is a leveraged bet.

"There is a lot more risk associated with long/short investing than many believe," he says. "And you have a lot more riding on the manager's skill than with someone running a large-cap growth fund, so you have to be a lot more careful about picking this type of fund manager."

"I don't think many institutional investors are taking the extra level of thoughtfulness that is required with these types of investments," he continues. "Although one can never be sure what is going on in someone else's organization from appearances, this seems to be the case."

One of the nice things about having so much money is the pension fund's ability to be aggressive about pushing down fees, asking a lot of questions, and being really nosy about how the fund is being managed.

"Some people do not want to do business with us because they think we're too involved in the operation," the managing director says.

Some hedge fund managers' egos do not allow for pushy investors. One hedge fund in particular has not been willing to negotiate its fees because it believes it can replace the pension fund's dollars with someone else's in a heartbeat—and at a higher fee.

"We have not pulled the money out of this fund because we are greedy and we want the returns," the managing director says. "Just because they don't want us does not mean we do not want them. This is totally a game of egos and if we can put our ego aside then we are going to make more money than another plan sponsor who cannot put their ego aside."

The pension fund speaks with its hedge fund managers on a monthly or bimonthly basis and it reviews the funds' performances and positions daily. If a questionable situation arises, the pension fund managers are quick to call to find out what is going on.

"We are always sort of checking ourselves, saying this is what the market is doing, this is what we expect from a manager, and this manager is not acting in sync with the thought, so we need to understand why," the managing director says.

The pension fund's managers believe that now is the time to expand its exposure to hedge funds.

"There has been a lot of learning going on in the industry with other people's money and many investors have been scared away, and the opportunity is right to expand our program," the managing director says. "It is up to us to go in and pick people that we think will be the best going forward."

Third-Party Marketers

Many believe that to be successful, hedge fund managers need two things: strong performance numbers and a pool of assets to manage. New managers and some experienced ones subscribe to the *Field of Dreams* theory: "If you build it, they will come" when it comes to raising money. Simply put, if the manager puts up good numbers, investors will flock from all over the world to give him or her money to manage. It does not work this way. A track record takes time, work, and energy, and often raising capital is something that managers leave to others.

"It is one of the hardest parts of the job," says one fund manager. "When I started my fund, I knew I could pick stocks and put up good numbers but I had no idea how to raise money, nor was it a skill I was interested in learning."

As the hedge fund industry has grown so has the business of raising money for funds. Gone are the days of fund managers relying solely on family and friends for the bulk of the assets they manage. Sure, most funds start out that way, but once things get going, managers need to look outside their circle to the world of wealthy individuals, family offices, and institutional investors. To reach these people, many fund managers team up with third-party marketers. These firms specialize in raising money for funds. For the most part, they receive a fee for the assets they raise as well as a trailing fee for however long that the capital and any new capital that their clients invest remains with the fund.

The world of potential investors is in reality much larger than it seems. As the stock market rallies, options are granted, companies are bought, and the economy stays strong, many more people and institutions become wealthy enough to meet the SEC's requirements needed to invest in hedge funds. Still, a hedge fund manager needs help in getting his or her story out, someone who has the databases and, more important, the relationships with investors.

Investors are looking for answers and fund managers are looking for assets, a third-party marketer that is doing its job can provide both.

Third-party marketers are not just brokers; the good ones provide a complete set of comprehensive services to hedge funds that include everything from capital raising and client relations to helping them set up a business and running the operation as well as development and review of all marketing material.

Most third-party marketers operate with the basic premise that their clients, in this case hedge fund managers, understand how to run a portfolio but do not have any idea how to run the actual marketing side of their operation and in turn have no idea how to raise assets. It seems that most managers start and finish the marketing process with their rolodex—this will only bear so much fruit. New and existing managers alike new to expand their universe of potential investors—they need to beyond an existing list of names and numbers. Managers also need to learn how to present their fund, strategy and investment team properly to potential investors and referrals partners—a good third-party marketing firm will help with all this as well.

Traditionally in the third-party marketing business, the hedge fund manager pays the marketer a small retainer and then a piece of the fees generated by any of the investors the marketer introduces to the fund. For example, if the marketer introduces an investor who puts $10 million into the fund, the payout would be as follows: A standard hedge fund fee structure is usually a 1 or 2 percent management fee and a 20 percent incentive fee. If the manager was up 10 percent they would be paid 20 percent of $1 million in new profits or $200,000 and a 1 percent management fee of $100,000. The marketer would receive 20 percent of both fees or $40,000 of the incentive fee and $20,000 of the management fee.

Third-party marketers as of this writing needed to be affiliated with a broker dealer and had to have securities licenses in order to get paid. The SEC and Congress as well as some state governments had been paying close attention to the third party marketing business and it appeared that in the Summer of 2010, as the Financial Reform Bill was being debated and signed into law by President Obama; that it may contain some new rules and regulations that would directy impact the third-party marketing business.

In talking to a few third-party marketers, they all seem to say that in their experience many fund managers tend to be singularly focused on the portfolio and have a hard time talking, walking, and in some cases dressing themselves, which together can present a real problem if the manager is trying to build a business and gain assets.

"We add value by taking the marketing and capital rasing away from them," said one third-party marketer based in New York. "Our job is to raise assets, theirs is to manage the portfolio. It is a good relationship."

Many hedge funds, regardless of assets under management and track record, use third-party marketers. There is no set size or experience level—most third-party marketers work with funds they believe that they can be successful with because they want to get paid for their efforts. Each fund manager has a different idea about investors but all have the same wants—the desire for more assets under management.

"Managers who have been out on their own for a while and see that things aren't clicking are the ones who are the most receptive to our advice and guidance," said a New York-based third-party marketer. "They realize that they are going to have to change in order to really grow and they look to us to help them build a more successful business."

Third-party marketing is not easy. It is a tough business. It is not respected by many and is something that few are good at over a long period of time. Issues come up, relationships don't work out and funds are not raised. If you are a fund manager looking to raise assets; do your homework—before hiring a third-party marketer. If you are an investor being pitched by a third-party marketer; ditto. Email me at das@hedgeanswers.com if you have questions.

An Individual Investor

While institutions invest enormous amounts of money in hedge funds and represent the bulk of dollars in the industry today, individual investors also play a significant role. Most of the large funds tend to have a mix of institutional and individual money, while many of the smaller funds—those under $300 million in assets—and usually consist solely of high-net-worth investors and family offices.

"When you start out, the first people you go to are friends and family and friends of your friends and family," says one hedge fund manager. "It is hard to attract an institutional audience and it is even harder to get them to invest in a new fund or even a relatively new fund with somewhat of a track record."

One manager told me that the bulk of the money that he used to launch his fund came from clients he had as a stockbroker at Lehman Brothers. "These people knew me, trusted me, and believed in my ability to pick stocks and make money," he says.

One individual who invests in hedge funds through a small family office is a doctor in Newport Beach, California. The doctor, who requested that his name not be published, told me his father had decided a number of years ago that the best way for the family to maintain its wealth would be to pool its resources into a family office.

"The family office allows us to take advantage of our belief in the efficient market theory," he says. "We believe that you need to look to alternative investments as potentially yielding a better rate of return with potentially the same if not lesser risk ratios."

The family office invests in a core group of funds that meet the needs of most of the family, while allowing individuals to invest in other funds, too. The idea is to make sure that everyone is provided for and that those who can tolerate risk do so and those who cannot do not. The doctor's mother, for example, who is 82, is in a core fund that all the family members invest in but she is also in a fixed-income fund with no one else in the family. Four nuclear families take part in the family office.

Over the years, the doctor has made some mistakes and has had to redeem out of a number of funds because they did not live up to his expectations. When a fund is not putting up the numbers he expects, he looks elsewhere for the returns. Currently they run five pools of assets: a core hedged equity portfolio, a PIPE portfolio, a commodities portfolio, a diversified equity portfolio, and a small fund of funds. Since they started managing their wealth this way, the portfolios have beaten the benchmarks but it has not been easy.

"We have had our ups and downs," he said. "It is very hard work and it is very labor intensive. Sometimes I wonder if I would have done just as well picking a fund of funds and letting them do all of the asset allocation."

In the core hedged equity portfolio, the doctor invests in mid-cap stocks. "Our mid-cap managers are not young guys that have not been around the block, and they invest very similarly to Warren Buffett. The fund consistently provides us with steady returns year after year. It is really a great fund for us," he says.

The doctor found the mid-cap stock managers after he decided that it was time to leave a private bank and look elsewhere for returns. "I basically ran spreadsheets on domestic equity managers and found that the fund was better than anybody else in performing in up and down markets," he says. "We found the other fund through a person we use as a sounding board for ideas who recommended it to us."

sharpe ratio

the ratio of return above the minimum acceptable return divided by the standard deviation. It provides information of the return per unit of dispersion risk.

The doctor, who also acts as the managing partner without pay, does most of the research to find fund managers. He reads everything he can get his hands on and speaks to brokers, advisers, and investors around the country. "Finding hedge fund managers is sort of a networking kind of thing," he says. "I found one manager when I read about him in a *Barron's* article. I called him to schmooze with him and we have become friends."

The doctor also fields calls from third-party marketers and brokers who are paid to raise money for funds. The doctor says it does not bother him when these people call because they often provide him with information. "You have to evaluate everything for yourself and you surely cannot take their word for it, but there is really no harm in talking to them," he says. "These people don't make money from my end of the transaction."

The doctor does all his own due diligence and he recommends funds to the family, but each member makes his or her own decision. For example, his sister has chosen not to go into the new core fund. Instead she is looking for an investment that will provide her with a steady stream of cash rather than superior returns year after year.

As the managing partner, he evaluates everything from track records and previous employment to *Sharpe ratios*, risk–reward ratios, and *standard deviations*. He is self-taught and learned almost everything he knows about finance from eight feet of financial books he keeps in his home. In some cases, he works with a few consultants and pays them a fee for investment advice.

standard deviation

a measure of the dispersion of a group of numerical values from the mean. It is calculated by taking the differences between each number in the group and the arithmetic average, squaring them to give the variance, summing them, and taking the square root.

"I keep extensive files and information on funds that we invest in currently and on those funds that we may invest with in the future," he says. "On average I probably spend less than four hours a week on following the funds. I spend more time worrying about individual stocks that I trade on my own than on how the funds are performing."

The doctor and his wife have invested in a fund that specializes in distressed securities, while the other family members have decided against it. "We chose to invest in a distressed fund because we believe it is a wiser thing to do than individual investments, because sometimes these things go belly-up," he says. "By being in the fund we are able to have 15 positions instead of three or four and are protected against the downturns."

The doctor runs the family office on a laptop computer that he uses to administer what he calls portfolios. These portfolios are either limited liability corporations or limited partnerships. Each of the portfolios, of which the family office has five, provides the members of the family access to specific funds.

"No one has ever gotten upset because an investment wasn't successful," he says. "What they do get upset about is when I don't get them performance figures as quickly as they think they should be made available."

For the most part, the doctor tends to stay away from the marquee names in the hedge fund world, instead looking for funds that he can grow with along with the manager.

"It is a small family office that allows us to invest tax efficiently and to find managers with good tax-efficient returns, in turn protecting and maintaining our wealth," he says. "We are not doing it for tax avoidance; we are doing it to make superior returns over time."

A Consulting Firm

When people ask which the best investment bank on Wall Street is, the answer is always, Goldman Sachs Group. It is the premier investment house in the world and, whether people admit it, the remaining Wall Street firms want to be like it. I believe that statement to be as true today in April of 2010 as it was five years ago, even with all the bad press, and negative comments coming out of Washington and many state capitals, Goldman Sachs is still the gold standard.

When it comes to hedge fund consultants the situation is not the same. There are many firms around the world that specialize in providing investment advice and guidance to investors on every single type of investment known and offered. There is not one that stands out among the rest of the pack—simply put there is no Goldman Sachs or better yet gold standard—there are many and each has something unique to offer.

The east coast, particularly the Greater Boston area is littered with companies that provide advice and counsel on picking hedge funds and creating portfolios. Many of the firms in the Boston area focus on providing their services directly to endowments and foundations. Massachusetts has a large number of schools and institutions with sizable endowments and all of them regardless of size and the complexity of their operation need some advice at some time.

Ten years ago, there were one or two firms that would have been considered to be the gold standard, but because there are so many firms out there doing the same thing, it just isn't true anymore. My experience is that many of these firms just don't operate ethically and often times do not fully disclose the extent of their relationships with the funds that they are recommended. More importantly, it seems that because the consulting firms seem to be a good first stop for many people, there seems to be a constant revolving door of employees—the educational curve is significant and I am not sure they add any real value to the equation.

My other concern is the lack of real due diligence and manager selection. One of the problems that the hedge fund industry had experienced in the years leading up to the credit crisis was that everyone wanted to invest in the same manager.

There was a significant amount of self protection or CYA in the vernacular at the operation that was transmitted to oardrooms around the globe when it came time to making decisions about where to put endowment money.

There was a time when a purchasing manager knew that buying certain products from certain companies even if they did not work right or performed as expected was the safe choice. "Nobody ever got fired for buying IBM—in short even if it did not work, jobs were secure. The same practice is employed by many board members and investment committees during the fund selection and asset allocation process."

"Its easy to choose a fund or a manager that everyone knows," said the investment director at a billion dollar endowment. "Names are more important than how the manager does it or how good they are at what they are supposed to be doing. If the big names are in the fund, well we should be in there as well; too many people think this way in the industry."

Following the herd is something that should not be done whether you are investing in a fund or anything else. Just because someone else is doing it does not mean it is right for you. I know it sounds simple, and you are thinking this is something that could never happen to me. Well, guess what, it can, and if you are not careful, it will.

Unfortunately, when it comes to consultants, many—too many in my opinion—follow the herd. There are a handful of consultants that simply take the easy way out and in the end I believe that hurts the investors. Investors need to get good, objective advice in order to act accordingly. However, when the presentation begins with "well this is what Harvard and Yale are doing," I believe there is a real problem.

That being said, there are some consultants that do a good job and I am not trying to indict the entire industry here, quite the opposite. What I am saying to you is that you should do your homework and complete a thorough due diligence review of the consultant before you engage them to help with portfolio construction.

Here is a list of questions that need to be answered:

- Describe the team and how it functions.
- Where does your knowledge about investment strategy come from?
- How often do you meet with managers?
- Describe your due diligence process.
- What is the greatest weakness of your organization and how do you compensate for it?

The answers to these questions should make sense to you. There are more to add, however, this is a good start. If you don't like what you hear, dig deeper.

In some, if not all cases, the relationship that you are establishing is your first line of defense/offense in the development and implementation of your portfolio and as such it needs to be strong and without holes. Get the questions answered—the answers should be thoughtful, to the point, without any nonsense. If not, well, do not hire the firm, simple as that. If you have questions about this process email me at das@hedgeanswers.com.

Consultants should consult. Their job is to provide you with independent advice and guidance. The firm should not earn money from the funds that they recommend and should as a matter of course provide a detailed explanation of any and all conflicts of interest and what if any affect it will have on the work that they are doing for you. In most cases, conflicts will not exist—but ask about them—because you need to be sure. During the due diligence process, it is important to establish the following five attributes of any consultant you are thinking about hiring to help you with portfolio creation:

1. No conflicts of interest
2. Should not manage money
3. Be fee based
4. Be objective
5. Have institutional memory

Firms that possess these five qualities are firms that are worth talking to further because they may be able to provide you with services you require in order to get the job done. More due diligence is needed but you are headed in the right direction.

It is important to understand how the consultant conducts research to find managers. Get a good understanding of how the work is done and by whom. The depth of the bench is important. Also, product knowledge is important. It is better to have a consultant that is a master of many products then an expert in one.

The tools that the consultant uses are also important. Many firms have developed a series of databases and research facilities to track investment managers, create portfolios, and monitor portfolios. Ask about these tools. Find out what they use, ask how often information is updated, and how the information is verified.

In light of Madoff and the other scandals of late, there has been an uptick in the number of firms that provide background checks on managers and firms. This is an important step that cannot be overlooked. Checking out a manager's background sounds simple and easy, but in today's society nothing is easy or simple. People lie about the dumbest things. One of the biggest lies that people tell is where they went to college and what they studied. It sounds silly but it happens all the time. If someone lies about the small things imagine what they are capable of lying about when things start getting tough—by the way, things always get tough....

Gathering the data is not all that complicated; it can be time consuming, but managers are willing to provide it because, well, they want your money. Your consultant should be able to get the data and help you process it. Ask them for detailed proposals for other clients. They can redact information so as not to violate confidentiality; it should not be a problem. Getting examples of their work product will help see just how thorough the consultant is and what you can expect from them.

"The problem is not gathering the data," said one consultant. "The problem is processing and preparing for clients. Often managers provide too much information especially when they know our client is an endowment or institution that is considering making an investment."

On the retail or individual side, consultants are more apt to be financial advisors and brokers who provide advice and guidance to would-be hedge fund investors. Many of the firms that work with institutional investors also work with individuals as well—it all comes down to assets.

The people who specialize in working with individuals are predominately wealth-managers—the new name for financial advisors and brokers. These people are for the most part well-intentioned, however, in most cases they are limited in both their product knowledge and ability to access funds. Most firms or advisor platforms allow brokers and advisors to use only funds that are pre-approved. These funds have gone through a vetting process and have passed a thorough due diligence. In some cases, funds will reduce the fees that they charge in order to get on the platform; in other situations the funds pay a fee to be on the platform. In either case, the client or individual investor is in some way, shape, or form paying for the privilege of being able to access the fund through his broker, wealth manager, financial advisor, or what have you. As long as the fees are discussed up front and there is no ambiguity, accessing hedge funds this way is a fine solution for many investors. If you go this route, make sure you understand the costs associated with the investment.

When it comes to choosing a consultant, whether it be for an individual or institution, it comes down to trust. If you believe the person or firm is going to work in your best interest and provide you with the advice, guidance, and support you need to make the best decision about your money and investments, hire them. But, remember this: do the work and make sure you get it right and spend at least the same amount time picking a consultant as you do a refrigerator....

A Manager of Managers

Although the rest of us eventually grow up and out of it, in the hedge fund world some people still like to hold their MOM's hand: that is, the hand of their manager of managers.

A manager of managers acts as an adviser to investors who are looking for a money manager but do not want to deal with the day-to-day responsibilities of managing those investments and do not want to go into individual hedge funds or a fund of funds.

A MOM will customize multimanager alternative investment strategies for institutional and high-net-worth investors. The strategies include the use of hedge funds, managed futures trades, and foreign exchange trades. Although MOMs have their fingers on the pulse of the markets, they do not try to time the markets. One of the benefits of using a MOM is that doing so provides the investors with both freedom and control over their investments—two characteristics that are rare in today's alternative investment world.

These organizations exert enormous amounts of control over the managers they invest with. The MOM usually requires the manager to sign a contract that details exactly what the manager can do with the money and provides for next-day redemption if the manager violates the contract. These organizations pick and choose individual money managers for their clients. The managers operate separate accounts for each investor. In most cases, an investor creates a portfolio of managers to handle all alternative investment needs.

One such MOM is a company called Parker Global Strategies LLC. Started by Virginia Parker in 1995, it currently has more than 15 employees in its headquarters in Stamford, Connecticut, has an office in Japan, and—since its inception—has advised on more than $1.75 billion.

"What makes us different from a fund of funds is that we are in control of what is going on with the money and the manager at all times," she says. "We tailor the contract with the manager according to what we are ready to do with the client's money. This means that we are always going to hire managers to run their strategy the way they typically run it. We don't want to ask them to do something they normally don't do or do something that may inversely impact their performance."

The contract that Parker signs with managers is very thorough. Not only does the contract describe the trading strategy in detail, but it also includes limits on leverage, value-at-risk limits, and which instruments the manager is allowed to trade, as well as a list of those the manager is allowed to use as a counterparty. "If, for example, options are an integral part of someone's strategy, then they may be eligible to one manager but not to another manager with whom we allocate," she says.

Not all managers are willing to succumb to the controls Parker and other MOMs place on them. Those who do seem to make it all worthwhile. "There are more than enough very, very good managers out there, which means that we can provide some real value-added to our clients," she says. "The reason managers have been willing to do this is that they respect the work we are trying to do for our clients and look at us as a source of capital that provides them access to many different sources of funds through one entity."

Once a manager is chosen, Parker's company monitors trading activity daily. The firm independently marks to market every trade daily, unless it is something fairly illiquid, in which case the position is marked to market weekly. Parker also runs the positions through a risk monitoring system and monitors the activity to ensure that it is following the trading policy specified in the contract.

In some cases, the MOM knows more about the manager's portfolio than the manager does. For example, a manager who does not use value-at-risk or stress-testing analysis may be able to learn something from Parker.

"It is not unusual on the risk side for our firm to know more than the manager on a quantitative basis," she says. "If managers do not know this information, it does not mean they are not good traders. All it means is that they probably did not work in a banking environment, at least not when those tools were becoming standard practices."

Parker likes to know what is going on with the manager. Although the firm is always looking for new managers, it primarily sticks with a core group of traders. Once she finds a manager she likes, she visits and asks the manager to complete a very detailed questionnaire. If Parker likes what she reads, the firm sends in a team of people to perform operational and risk-management due diligence. The team looks at the manager's accounting practices, systems, and models, and checks references.

"Then we try to negotiate a contract with the manager," she says.

In 2005, Parker was tracking more than 2,000 managers both large and small in multiple investment styles and strategies in its proprietary database. It is not unusual for Parker and her staff to speak with the firm's clients and managers every day.

"We have a very high degree of comfort with most of our managers," she says. "Our philosophy is that once we find a good manager that still has capacity, we want to be the ones to use that capacity rather than just go try to find more and more managers."

In almost every instance Parker has the traders manage money for her clients in a separate account, but it has gone into a third-party fund a couple of times. Then the manager must meet specific requirements, including 100 percent transparency and next-day redemption capability.

Parker says that because of the amount of information and control she requires, there needs to be a lot of trust and a lot of both sides wanting to work together. "This is a relationship business, and we like to focus on relationships that are working well," she says.

In 2005, the firm was managing $500 million, a large portion of which was with managers. The firm did maintain a significant cash position to fund a guaranteed structure that it manages. For the most part, Parker's clients are banks and the customers of banks. The company manages the banks' own capital, while for their customers it creates private-label products that are marketed directly to institutions and corporations. The firm is paid both a management fee and a performance fee.

Parker also operates the first publicly registered and largest hedge fund in Japan. Marketed as a closed-end fund through IBJ Securities, it was started in March 1998 and requires a minimum investment of $1,000. Its shares do not trade in a public market.

When it comes to picking managers to work with, Parker likes to rely on word of mouth and her experience. She talks to people who allocate large sums of money, asking them whom they know, whom they see, and most important whom they like.

"I have never been able to find a manager in a database," she says. "In my experience having a database is the least important element in finding good managers."

Parker uses a network of large banks and insurance companies as well as people who have been in the industry for years to get information and ideas on managers. "There is a lot of camaraderie in the industry, and I think that a lot of people have a vested interest in giving each other tips on who is hot and who is not and try to help keep people out of trouble," she says. "There is a lot of very good information that is shared that is not readily available."

If Parker finds that a manager is not complying with the contract, she can end the relationship. Although it has never happened (most managers fix problems when they are told they are not in compliance), it is an aspect of the business that makes it unique in the alternative investment world.

The return clients receive ranges from 10 percent to 30 percent, depending on the strategy being used. Parker uses traders that employed strategies ranging from global macro and convertible arbitrage to U.S. and European stock long/short and managed futures.

Her company has stayed away from a number of strategies because of their risk, Parker says, explaining why the firm uses managers employing high-yield, emerging markets, and mortgage strategies.

"We do have a couple of managers that we like in high-yield and we were ready to allocate and decided not to this summer because of what was happening in the market," she says. "We are not quite ready to allocate to these strategies but do plan on going to them in the future."

Parker believes that being a manager of managers offers much more control than being a fund of funds operator. She says that she knows of a lot of smart fund of funds managers who found that a number of their managers were going to markets outside their normal routine and they wanted to redeem. These managers put in their redemption notices and by the time they could redeem, the assets were gone—all lost.

"When you operate a fund of funds, you have no control," she says. "Even to be a fund of funds manager with 100 percent transparency, you don't have control if you can't get out, so what good does it do you?

"Our way allows us access to invest possibly with the same managers, but we are able to do it on our terms," she continues. "At the moment there are plenty of good managers that are willing to take money on our terms and therefore we have a business model that we like a lot."

Typically, Parker and her staff try to follow the market and get an understanding of what is going on, not in an effort to time the market but in an effort to stay out of trouble.

"Our views on the markets can cause us to have some small shifts in allocations but typically not huge, dramatic swings," she says. "Ultimately, the allocations are my call, but the principals here work together, talk, and share views, and usually we come up with a consensus on which we base our decision."

Parker believes in light of the carnage many hedge fund investors felt in the wake of the collapse of the equity markets over the last few years, people have now come to understand the value of risk management systems and in turn diversification.

"We have had a number of successful years when others did not," she says. "It was because we had the control, which meant that we had the capability not to be allocating in some places and very quickly shift allocations to a few managers who had good performance during those periods. Our control really made a huge difference."

Conclusion

To invest in hedge funds or not to invest in hedge funds, that seemed to be the question on the minds of investors around the globe in the wake of the credit crisis. For the last three years, Congress and President Obama have wanted more regulation, the Securities and Exchange Commission wanted to be taken seriously, and managers wanted to increase assets under management in order to continue run their businesses—it has been a glorious time to be in the industry.

I do not recall a time in the fifteen plus years that I have been working in the hedge fund industry, that I have ever witnessed so many people, places, and things being focused on these sorts of investment vehicles. From insider trading scandals to the case against Goldman Sachs, it seems like every day the phone rings with stories about funds in trouble, bringing in large assets, or just going out of business. The hedge fund industry, while large in terms of assets under management, is really a small place. People do not want to hear of a fund manager going out of business or someone who sustained enormous losses, even if they are vying for the same investors and in some cases the same investments. The industry is closely knit, from the accountants and lawyers to the prime brokers and the traders to the fund managers and the investors. People know each other, like each other—for the most part, and want to see the industry continue to grow and thrive. Make no mistake—hedge funds are here to stay. The industry has many, many years of success ahead of it.

Unfortunately, the usual story in the press about hedge funds shows something else: wealthy people investing with a secretive fund manager to earn enormous amounts of money and living lavishly and happily ever after. Every now and then there is a story about excesses like the helicopter to work or the 50 cars coupled with the huge shopping sprees or the weird artwork.

It has been the art and real estate purchases by some managers that have been making headlines as of late. There are very few positive stories written about the hedge fund industry. Since the fall of 2009, the papers have been littered with stories of the insider trading investigations and indictments. These situations were still playing out in early 2010 and looked to be for quite some time. The stories are fascinating to read. And while the outcome of some of the indictments was still unknown, the guilty should pay for their crimes. But remember, one bad apple does not spoil the bunch.

These and other stories are very hard for the average person to relate to, let alone the sophisticated investor. Money and markets are not everything; however, stories play on jealousy, while exposing greed and making most people long for the wealth and privileged life that hedge fund investors and managers seem to have. These stories sizzle, and sizzle sells.

Well, here is a story with an entirely different spin that came out in the wake of the near collapse of Long-Term Capital. It is an oldie but a goodie, in that it has appeared in the other two editions of this book.

On December 23, 1998, I had a message on my answering machine from Paul Wong, the Midas trader who runs Edgehill Capital in Old Greenwich, Connecticut. The message said, "Dan, call me—I have an interesting story to tell you." I figured that the story had to do with Long-Term Capital. Earlier in the day, the story broke that Meriwether and his partners stood to make a small fortune from their performance in the fourth quarter. I figured Wong was going to give me some color on the situation. I was completely wrong. When Wong and I finally spoke on December 24, he told me one of the greatest stories about hedge funds that I have ever heard.

In 1993, Wong got a call from the brother of a boyhood friend. The gentleman called Wong in desperation. It seemed that he had been doing some math and realized that the money he had been saving for his daughter's college education would be nowhere near what he needed. His brother suggested that he call Wong and ask for help. When the two spoke, Wong told the gentleman about the hedge fund he was starting and that he thought it would make sense for him to put his daughter's education money to work there. The father agreed, figuring that if Wong was putting his own money in the fund, it was as good a place as any for his money. He invested $45,000 as one of Edgehill's first investors. He had good years, like 1995 (up 134 percent) and 1996 (up 24 percent), and a bad year in 1997 (down 7 percent). Edgehill was up over 41 percent in 1998, and through the first six months of 1999 the fund was up 10 percent. The fund closed to investors in 2004 after not recovering from the tech bubble.

Throughout it all, the gentleman stayed with Wong. Toward the end of December 1998, Wong got a call from the father, explaining that he would need the money the following fall to pay his daughter's tuition at the University of New Hampshire. Although he was not surprised because he had been following the performance all along, he was quite happy. On December 24, 1998, his $45,000 had grown to over $125,000, enough to pay his daughter's college tuition and then some.

"Everyone thinks that hedge funds are about greed," said Wong. "In reality, hedge funds are about providing people with capital to do things that are important to them. What better reason to go to work every day than to know that the money you make is going to provide for a child's education?"

This story is not unique. There are many cases where fund managers and investors have used the proceeds of their investments to do great things. Many of the world's greatest philanthropists are hedge fund managers. There have been countless stories about the generosity of people like George Soros, Michael Steinhardt, Paul Tudor Jones, and Julian Robertson who have given away and continue to give away hundreds of millions of dollars to help those less fortunate and work very hard to make this world a better place. Generosity is something that flows from the hedge fund industry to literally every corner of the globe.

A dear friend of mine who shall remain nameless spends hundreds of thousands of dollars each year to provide a carnival at his home in New Jersey, complete with hot dogs, face painting, corn on the cob, a Ferris wheel, and jet ski rides to hundreds of underprivileged children from New York City. He doesn't ask for anything in return except that the kids and their families have a good time and enjoy themselves.

Alfred Winslow Jones, the father of the industry, did not live a lavish life, but instead gave a lot of his money away, helping to make New York a better place to live. The list of hedge fund managers and investors who do good things around the world with their wealth goes on and on.

Hedge funds do not destroy markets or ruin the economies of countries. Hedge funds are investment vehicles that seek significant returns regardless of market conditions. Managers are paid handsomely when they make those returns and next to nothing if they fail. It is a win-win situation for both investors and managers. The managers' money is truly where their mouths are, unlike mutual fund managers who get paid regardless of how they perform.

The problem comes when the managers step out-of-bounds and make mistakes. Then it is for the investor and the manager to determine how best to solve the problem. In most cases, the investors will redeem. If there is fraud, the manager should pay and be brought to justice.

The idea of government influence, intervention, and regulation is not the end-all, be-all solution to the so-called hedge fund problem. It is questionable what, if anything, regulation can do to help the industry and its investors and more importantly the capital markets. The more government involvement, the worse things will be in my opinion. Members of Congress, and government regulators, who have very little knowledge of money and markets, should stay away from blanket regulations without fully understanding the impact of the laws on the industry and its investors. Sweeping statements from Committee chairs in order to insight constituents is not something that does any good. Instead of finger pointing and blame, there needs to be thoughtful discussion. However, this is not what gets politicians the headlines or reelected.

It is silly to think that one should put all of their assets in investments that only make money when the markets rise. Hedge funds in theory should provide a tool for investors to make money regardless of which markets are moving. The problem is that investors need to take the time and responsibility to perform the due diligence and make sure what they think they are investing in, is what they are actually getting. Due diligence is important and cannot be overlooked.

In a capitalist society, we subscribe to the theory that markets correct themselves when errors occur. If the market deems a hedge fund or the entire hedge fund industry too risky, too expensive, or no longer avalid investment choice, then the market will force a change, and the industry will adapt or go away. I don't see that happening, but I also never would have guessed that Lehman Brothers would go bankrupt or Bear Stearns would be forced to be sold. So stay tuned, pay attention, and get involved. This ride is far from over.

Appendix A

Hedge Fund Strategies

The following list defines a number of hedge fund styles and strategies that are being used by managers around the globe. The information was compiled by Hedgefund.net.*

Capital Structure Arbitrage A relative value fund that attempts to capture pricing inefficiencies among various tranches of debt or equity of the same or related companies.

Convertible Arbitrage Manager focuses on obtaining returns with low or no correlation to the market. Manager buys different securities of the same issuer (e.g., the common stock and convertibles) and works the spread between them. For example, within the same company the manager buys one form of security that he believes is undervalued and sells short another security of the same company.

Country Specific Manager focuses on a single country, or a few countries from a specific region. Russia- and Japan-focused funds have been popular in the last few years.

CTA / Managed Futures CTA is short for Commodity Trading Advisor. CTAs generally trade commodity futures, options, and foreign exchange, and most are highly leveraged.

*2010 by Channel Capital Group Inc. Reprinted with permission.

Distressed Buying the equity or debt of companies that are in or facing bankruptcy. Manager hopes to buy company securities at a low price and that the company will come out of bankruptcy and the securities will appreciate.

Emerging Markets Manager focuses on investing in the securities of companies from emerging or developing countries.

Energy Sector Manager is primarily invested in securities revolving around the energy sector.

Event-Driven Manager takes a significant position in a limited number of companies with special situations: companies' situations are unusual in a possible variety of ways and offer profit opportunities; for example, depressed stock, event in offing offering significant potential market interest (e.g. company is being merged with or acquired by another company), reorganizations, bad news emerging that will temporarily depress stock (so manager shorts stock), and so on.

Finance Sector Manager is primarily invested in securities revolving around the finance sector, including banks, brokerages, and so on.

Fixed Income (non arbitrage) Manager invests in fixed income instruments, either long, short, or both. Often employing a significant amount of leverage.

Fixed Income Arbitrage Manager generally plays the spread between similar fixed income securities. Often highly leveraged.

Fund of Funds (Single Strategy) Fund of funds that invests only in one type of single strategy manager. For example, a fund of funds that invests only in convertible arbitrage would have fund of funds (single strategy) be their primary strategy and convertible arbitrage as their secondary strategy.

Fund of Funds (Market Neutral) Fund of funds that targets near zero correlation to the market or invests exclusively in market neutral or arbitrage strategies.

Fund of Funds (Multi-Strategy) Fund of funds that invests in a basket of different strategies.

Healthcare Sector Manager is primarily invested in securities revolving around the healthcare sector, including biotechnology.

Long Only Similar to a mutual fund, except the manager can trade a variety of financial instruments and use leverage to increase returns.

Long/Short Equity Also know as the Jones Model. Managers buy securities they believe will go up in price and sells short securities they believe will decline in price. Managers will be either net long or net short and may change their net position frequently. For example, a manager may be 60 percent long and 100 percent short, giving him a market exposure of 40 percent net short. The basic belief behind this strategy is that it will enhance the manager's stock- picking ability and protect investors in all market conditions.

Macro The investment philosophy is based on shifts in global economies. Derivatives are often used to speculate on currency and interest-rate moves.

Market Neutral Equity Any strategy that attempts to eliminate market risk and be profitable in any market condition.

Market Timer Manager attempts to time the market by allocating assets among investments primarily switching between mutual funds and money markets.

Mortgages A single-strategy hedge fund that primarily invests in mortgage-backed or mortgage-related securities.

Multi-Strategy A single hedge fund that runs several different strategies in-house that contribute to the total performance of the fund. Multi-strategy is different than a fund of funds (multi-strategy) in that the money is kept in-house as opposed to being farmed out to external managers.

Options Strategies A loosely defined category that describes any manager that focuses on options.

Other Arbitrage A relative value strategy that does not fall into any of the other categories. For example, dividend reinvestment arbitrage.

Regulation D The manager will make private investments in public companies in need of financing. Generally the manager will receive a discounted convertible note in return for a capital allocation, essentially locking in a profit.

Merger/Risk Arbitrage Also known as merger arbitrage. The manager invests in event-driven situations, such as leveraged buy-outs, mergers, and hostile takeovers. Managers purchase stock in the firm being taken over and, in some situations, sell short the stock of the acquiring company.

Short Bias Any manager who consistently has a net short exposure to the market. This category also includes short-only funds.

Short-Term Trading Manager focuses on short duration, opportunistic trades. Sometimes this strategy will include day trading.

Small/Micro Cap Usually long biased, the manager will exclusively focus on small and micro cap stocks.

Special Situations Special situations may broadly consist of some type of event-driven strategy. Managers will opportunistically trade in any type of security that they deem to be a special situation.

Statistical Arbitrage Believing that equities behave in a way that is mathematically describable, managers perform a low-risk, market-neutral analytical equity strategy. This approach captures momentary pricing aberrations in the stocks being monitored. The strategy's profit objective is to exploit mispricings in as risk-free a manner as possible.

Technology Sector Manager is primarily invested in securities revolving around the technology sector such as Internet, semiconductors, hardware, software, and so on.

Example of Material Included in an Onshore Document

The material included in this appendix has been supplied by Ron Geffner, partner in charge of the hedge fund practice at the New York–based law firm Sadis & Goldberg LLP. The blanks are to be filled in by the manager prior to launch.

Overview

Description of Interests and Structure

[ ] ("**Partnership**"), a limited partnership organized under the Delaware Revised Uniform Limited Partnership Act ("**Partnership Act**"), is offering limited partnership interests in the Partnership ("**Interests**") in a private placement pursuant to Section 4(2) of the Securities Act of 1933, as amended ("**Securities Act**"), and Regulation D promulgated thereunder. Generally, only persons who are Accredited Investors and Qualified Clients (as such terms are defined under the federal securities laws) may purchase Interests.

The Partnership was formed to pool investment funds of its investors (each a "**Limited Partner**" and, collectively, "**Limited Partners**;" and the General Partner (as defined below) together with Limited Partners shall be referred to as "**Partners**") to be managed by a number of investment managers selected by the General Partner ("**Managers**"). The minimum investment amount is $ [ ], although the General Partner has discretion to accept lesser amounts. Generally, new Limited Partners will be admitted on the first day of each month and withdrawals are on a quarterly basis, subject to a one-year lock-up and certain other restrictions. The Limited Partners, by pooling their assets in the Partnership, will be able to indirectly invest their funds in various portfolios of securities managed by various Managers. In the absence of a pooling vehicle such as the Partnership, an investor would not ordinarily be able to achieve the same degree of diversification or monitor, evaluate, and implement the same investment strategies as the Partnership.

[ ], a Delaware limited liability company is the general partner of the Partnership ("**General Partner**") and is responsible for the management of the Partnership, has discretionary investment authority over its assets, and is responsible for the day-to-day administration of the Partnership's affairs. The General Partner is registered as an investment adviser with the State of [ ] as the managing member and controlling person of the General Partner, [ ] controls all of the Partnership's operations and activities, and is primarily responsible for the management of the Partnership's portfolio.

Investment Objective and Strategy

The Partnership's investment objective is to seek to provide investors with consistent and superior long-term capital appreciation in all market conditions while also attempting to preserve capital and mitigate risk. In an attempt to achieve the Partnership's investment objective, the General Partner intends to invest its assets with a number of Managers. Each of these Managers is expected to have a disciplined policy for risk management and internal controls and may employ investment strategies involving the purchase and sale of stocks, bonds, and other debt securities, options, warrants, currencies, futures contracts, commodities (including precious metals), derivatives, partnership interests, money market instruments, and other ownership interests and indebtedness and may utilize a variety of specialized investment techniques. There are no limitations as to what types of investments the Partnership or the Managers may make. No assurance can be given, however, that the Partnership will achieve its investment objective, and investment results may vary substantially over time and from period to period. See "INVESTMENT PROGRAM."

Fees and Expenses

In consideration for its services, the General Partner receives a [ ] % monthly (approximately [ ] % annually) management fee based on the Partnership's net assets. In addition, the General Partner receives an annual performance allocation of [ ] % of the Partnership's net profits attributable to each Limited Partner, but only to the extent that such profits are in excess of (A) cumulative unrecovered losses carried forward from prior years based on a "high water mark" formula, and (B) a [ ] % hurdle rate, as further described under "SUMMARY OF OFFERING AND PARTNERSHIP TERMS." The Partnership will pay for its organizational and operating expenses including, but not limited to, all accounting, auditing, tax preparation, legal, administration, research, and trading costs, except that organizational expenses will be amortized over a period of 60 months, provided that such capitalization and amortization will not result in the qualification of the Partnership's financial statements. The General Partner will pay for its own administrative and overhead expenses incurred in connection with providing services to the Partnership.

Risk Factors, Conflicts of Interests, and Other Considerations

Before purchasing an Interest in the Partnership, you should carefully consider various risk factors and conflicts of interest, as well as suitability requirements, restrictions on transfer and withdrawal of Interests, and various legal, tax, and other considerations, all of which are discussed elsewhere in this Memorandum. Some of these considerations are set forth in the following section under the heading "IMPORTANT GENERAL CONSIDERATIONS." **An investment in the Interests offered by the Partnership should be viewed as a non-liquid investment and involves a high degree of risk. You should consider a subscription to purchase Interests only if you have carefully read this Memorandum.**

The Partnership is not registered as an investment company and is not subject to the investment restrictions, limitations on transactions with affiliates, and other provisions of the Investment Company Act of 1940, as amended ("**Investment Company Act**"), in reliance upon Section 3(c)(1) of the Investment Company Act, an exemption for an entity which has fewer than 100 beneficial owners of its securities. Accordingly, the Partnership will limit the number of beneficial owners of Interests and the percentage Interests of the Partnership acquired by certain Limited Partners.

The General Partner is not registered as a commodity pool operator under the Commodity Exchange Act ("**CEA**") based upon an exemption available under Rule 4.13(a)(3) promulgated pursuant to the CEA by the Commodity Futures Trading Commission ("**CFTC**"). The General Partner is registered as an investment adviser with the State of [ ]. A copy of Part II of the General Partner's Form ADV is attached hereto as Exhibit "C."

Important General Considerations

You should not construe the contents of this Memorandum as legal, tax, or investment advice and, if you acquire an Interest, you will be required to make a representation to that effect. You should review the proposed investment and the legal, tax, and other consequences thereof with your own professional advisors. The purchase of an Interest involves certain risks and conflicts of interest between the General Partner and the Partnership. See "RISK FACTORS AND CONFLICTS OF INTEREST." The General Partner reserves the right to refuse any subscription for any reason.

In making an investment decision, you must rely on your own examination of the Partnership and the terms of the offering of Interests, including the merits and risks involved. You and your representative(s), if any, are invited to ask questions and obtain additional information from the General Partner concerning the terms and conditions of the offering, the Partnership, and any other relevant matters to the extent the General Partner possesses such information or can acquire it without unreasonable effort or expense.

Neither the Securities Exchange Commission ("SEC") nor any state securities commission has passed upon the merits of participating in the Partnership, nor has the SEC or any state securities commission passed upon the adequacy or accuracy of this Memorandum. Any representation to the contrary is a criminal offense. The General Partner anticipates that: (i) the offer and sale of the Interests will be exempt from registration under the Securities Act and the various state securities laws; (ii) the Partnership will not be registered as an investment company under the Investment Company Act pursuant to an exemption provided by Section 3(c)(1) thereunder; and (iii) the General Partner will not be registered as a commodity pool operator under the CEA. Consequently, you will not be entitled to certain protections afforded by those statutes. The General Partner is registered as an investment adviser with the State of [ ].

Although the Partnership's investment strategy includes investing with Managers and investment funds that trade in financial futures and commodities as well as in options thereon, the General Partner is not registered with the CFTC as a commodity pool operator under the CEA. Pursuant to CFTC Rule 4.13, the General Partner is exempt from registration as a commodity pool operator and, therefore, the General Partner is not required to deliver a disclosure document and a certified annual report to participants in the Partnership. The Partnership qualifies for the foregoing exemption under CFTC Rule 4.13(a)(3) and Appendix A to Part 4 of the CFTC Rules based on the General Partner's undertaking to limit the Partnership's commodity trading activity so that at all times (A) with respect to investments with Managers, no more than 50% of the Partnership's assets will be allocated to Managers who trade commodity interests, and (B) with respect to the Partnership's direct trading activities, either (i) the aggregate initial margin and premiums required to establish commodity interest positions, determined at the time the most recent position was established, shall not exceed [ ]% of the liquidation value of the Partnership's portfolio after taking into account unrealized profits and losses on any such positions; or (ii) the aggregate net notional value of the Partnership's commodity interest positions, determined at the time the most recent position was established, shall not exceed 100% of the liquidation value of the Partnership's portfolio after taking into account unrealized profits and losses on any such positions.

As a Limited Partner, you may withdraw from the Partnership and receive payment for your Interests subject to a one year lock-up period and certain other restrictions as specified in the Limited Partnership Agreement of the Partnership ("Partnership Agreement"), a copy of which is annexed hereto as Exhibit A.

The offering of Interests is made only by delivery of a copy of this Memorandum to the person whose name appears hereon. The offering is made only to Accredited Investors and Qualified Clients, subject to certain exceptions. This Memorandum may not be reproduced, either in whole or in part, without the prior express written consent of the General Partner. By accepting delivery of this Memorandum, you agree not to reproduce or divulge its contents and, if you do not purchase any Interests, to return this Memorandum and the exhibits attached hereto to the General Partner.

Notwithstanding any provision in this Memorandum to the contrary, prospective Limited Partners (and their employees, representatives, and other agents) may disclose to any and all persons the U.S. federal income tax treatment and tax structure of the Interests offered hereby. For this purpose, "tax structure" is limited to facts relevant to the U.S. federal income tax treatment of the Interests, and does not include information relating to the identity of the issuer, its affiliates, agents, or advisors.

There is no public market for the Interests nor is any expected to develop. Even if such a market develops, no distribution, resale, or transfer of an Interest will be permitted except in accordance with the provisions of the Securities Act, the rules and regulations promulgated thereunder, any applicable state securities laws, and the terms and conditions of the Partnership Agreement. Any transfer of an Interest by a Limited Partner, public or private, will require the consent of the General Partner. Accordingly, if you purchase an Interest, you will be required to represent and warrant that you have read this Memorandum and are aware of and can afford the risks of an investment in the Partnership for an indefinite period of time. You will also be required to represent that you are acquiring the Interest for your own account, for investment purposes only, and not with any intention to resell or transfer all or any part of the Interest. This investment is suitable for you only if you have adequate means of providing for your current and future needs, have no need for liquidity in this investment, and can afford to lose the entire amount of your investment.

Although this Memorandum contains summaries of certain terms of certain documents, you should refer to the actual documents (copies of which are attached hereto or are available from the General Partner) for complete information concerning the rights and obligations of the parties thereto. All such summaries are qualified in their entirety by the terms of the actual documents. No person has been authorized to make any representations or furnish any information with respect to the Partnership or the Interests, other than the representations and information set forth in this Memorandum or other documents or information furnished by the General Partner upon request, as described above.

No rulings have been sought from the Internal Revenue Service ("IRS") with respect to any tax matters discussed in this Memorandum. You are cautioned that the views contained herein are subject to material qualifications and subject to possible changes in regulations by the IRS or by Congress in existing tax statutes or in the interpretation of existing statutes and regulations.

The information contained herein is current only as of the date hereof and you should not, under any circumstances, assume that there has not been any change in the matters discussed herein since the date hereof.

Summary of Offering and Partnership Terms

The following summary is qualified in its entirety by other information contained elsewhere in this Memorandum and by the Partnership Agreement. You should read this entire Memorandum and the Partnership Agreement carefully before making any investment decision regarding the Partnership and should pay particular attention to the information under the heading "RISK FACTORS AND CONFLICTS OF INTEREST." In addition, you should consult your own advisors in order to understand fully the consequences of an investment in the Partnership.

The Partnership [ ] ("Partnership") is a Delaware limited partnership, which commenced operations in [ ]. The Partnership operates as a pooled investment vehicle through which the assets of its Partners are managed by a number of investment managers selected by the General Partner ("Managers").

Management [ ], a Delaware limited liability company and investment adviser registered with the State of [ ], is the general partner of the Partnership ("General Partner") and is responsible for the management and investment decisions of the Partnership and the day-to-day administration of the Partnership's affairs. As the managing member and controlling person of the General Partner, [ ] controls all of the Partnership's operations and activities and is primarily responsible for the management of the Partnership's portfolio. See "MANAGEMENT."

The Offering The Partnership is offering limited partnership interests in the Partnership ("Interests") to persons who are Accredited Investors (as such term is defined in Rule 501 of Regulation D under the Securities Act) and Qualified Clients (as such term is defined in Rule 205-3 (d)(1) of the Investment Advisers Act of 1940, as amended ("Advisers Act")), subject to certain exceptions. Each Interest represents a percentage interest in the Partnership proportionate to the amount invested by each Partner in relation to the aggregate amount invested by all Partners.

Marketing Fees and Sales Charges. The General Partner may sell Interests through broker-dealers, placement agents, and other persons, and pay a marketing fee or commission in connection with such activities, including ongoing payments, at the General Partner's own expense. In certain cases, the General Partner and its affiliates reserve the right to pay a one-time fee or sales charge, on a fully disclosed basis, to a broker-dealer or placement agent based upon the capital contribution of the investor introduced to the Partnership by such broker-dealer or agent. Any such sales charge would be assessed against the referred investor and would reduce the amount actually invested by the investor in the Partnership.

How to Subscribe Attached as Exhibit B to this Memorandum are the subscription documents and instructions for subscribing ("Subscription Documents"). In order to subscribe for Interests, you must complete the Subscription Documents and return them to the Partnership. You must pay one hundred percent (100%) of your investment at the time you subscribe. Payment may be made by wire transfer of immediately available funds, or by a check payable to the Partnership. If you pay by check, your subscription will not be effective until the check has cleared and we receive payment on the check. To ensure compliance with applicable laws, regulations, and other requirements relating to money laundering, the General Partner may require additional information to verify the identity of any person who subscribes for an interest in the Partnership.

The General Partner, in its sole discretion, may accept securities in-kind as payment of your investment. *Any person who contributes securities in lieu of cash to the Partnership should consult with such person's counsel or advisors as to the tax effect of such contribution.*

Eligible Investors and Suitability

In order to invest in the Partnership, you must meet certain minimum suitability requirements, including qualifying as an "Accredited Investor" under the Securities Act and a "Qualified Client" under the Advisers Act, unless otherwise determined by the General Partner. The Subscription Documents set forth in detail the definition of Accredited Investor and Qualified Client. You must check the appropriate places in the Subscription Documents to represent to the Partnership that you are both an Accredited Investor and Qualified Client in order to be able to purchase Interests. The General Partner may reject any person's subscription for any reason or for no reason.

Accredited Investors are generally individuals with a net worth of more than $1,000,000 or who meet certain income thresholds, and entities with assets of at least $5,000,000. Generally, Qualified Clients are persons or companies that have either at least $750,000 under management with the General Partner immediately after investing, or have a net worth at the time of investing in excess of $1,500,000. The General Partner, in its discretion, may admit a limited number of non-Accredited Investors who have close relationships with the General Partner and who meet certain other requirements under the federal securities laws.

Under Regulation D, you may be required to appoint a "purchaser representative" in order to assist in evaluating the merits of investing in the Partnership. Each prospective investor who proposes to engage a purchaser representative must, prior to or concurrently with that investor's subscription, have completed and returned to the General Partner a Purchaser Representative Questionnaire, available on request from the General Partner. The General Partner will notify the prospective investor as to the acceptability of that person as a purchaser representative. A prospective investor should not, however, rely on the General Partner to determine the qualifications of any proposed purchaser representative.

The suitability standards referred to herein represent minimum suitability requirements for persons seeking to invest in the Partnership, and, accordingly, just because you satisfy such standards does not necessarily mean that the Interests are a suitable investment for you.

Entities subject to the Employee Retirement Income Security Act of 1974, as amended ("ERISA"), and other tax-exempt entities may purchase Interests. However, investment in the Partnership by such entities requires special consideration. Trustees or administrators of such entities should consult their own legal and tax advisers. See "ERISA CONSIDERATIONS."

Minimum Investment

The minimum initial investment (or capital contribution) that will be accepted from a new Limited Partner is $[ ] although the General Partner has discretion to accept lesser amounts. There is no minimum or maximum aggregate amount of funds that may be contributed by all Partners to the Partnership. Limited Partners are not required to make any additional capital contributions to the Partnership. The General Partner, in its sole discretion, can accept or reject any initial subscriptions from prospective Limited Partners and any additional capital contributions from existing Limited Partners.

Admission of Limited Partners

Capital contributions generally will be accepted as of the first day of each month, however, the General Partner, in its sole discretion, has the right to admit new Limited

Partners and to accept additional funds from existing Limited Partners at any time. Upon such admission or receipt of additional capital contributions, the Interests of the Partners will be readjusted in accordance with their capital accounts.

In connection with an additional capital contribution by an existing Limited Partner, the General Partner may (i) treat such additional capital contribution as a capital contribution with respect to one of such Limited Partner's existing capital accounts or (ii) establish a new capital account to which such capital contribution shall be credited and which shall be maintained for the benefit of such Limited Partner separately from any existing capital account of such Limited Partner. Such separate capital account will be maintained for purposes of calculating the applicable Performance Allocation (as defined below). All funds invested in the Partnership by Limited Partners will be held in the Partnership's name, and the Partnership will not commingle its funds with any other party.

Withdrawals

Limited Partner Withdrawals. Limited Partners may not make any withdrawals from their capital accounts for a period of twelve (12) months after their investment in the Partnership ("Lock-Up Period"). After the expiration of the Lock-Up Period, Limited Partners may withdraw a minimum of $[ ] as of the last day of any calendar quarter (each such date shall be referred to herein as a "Withdrawal Date"), upon at least ninety (90) calendar days prior written notice to the General Partner, and in such other amounts and at such other times as the General Partner may determine in its sole discretion. Unless the General Partner consents, partial withdrawals may not be made if they would reduce a Limited Partner's capital account balance below $[ ]. All withdrawals shall be deemed made prior to the commencement of the following calendar quarter. The General Partner believes (but cannot guarantee) that the assets of the Partnership will be invested in a manner that would allow the General Partner to satisfy withdrawal requests. The Partnership has the right to pay cash or securities in-kind, or both, to a Limited Partner that makes a withdrawal from such Limited Partner's capital account.

If the General Partner in its discretion permits a Limited Partner to withdraw capital other than on a Withdrawal Date, the General Partner may impose an additional administrative fee to cover the legal, accounting, administrative, and any other costs and expenses associated with such withdrawal. Other than the administrative fee that may be imposed on withdrawals other than on a permitted Withdrawal Date, there are no withdrawal fees associated with a Limited Partner's withdrawal of capital from the Partnership.

Payments. A Limited Partner who requests a withdrawal of less than ninety percent (90%) of the value of such Limited Partner's capital account shall normally be paid within forty-five (45) calendar days after the applicable Withdrawal Date. A Limited Partner who is withdrawing ninety percent (90%) or more of the value of such Limited Partner's capital account in the aggregate within any fiscal year shall normally be paid ninety percent (90%) of an amount estimated by the General Partner to be the amount to which the withdrawing Limited Partner is entitled (calculated on the basis of unaudited data) within forty-five (45) calendar days after the applicable Withdrawal Date. The balance of the amount remaining in a withdrawing Limited Partner's capital account (subject to audit adjustments) shall be paid, without interest, within fifteen (15) calendar days after completion of the December 31 audited financial statements for the fiscal year in which the withdrawal occurs. The balance remaining will not be considered to be invested in the Partnership. Upon withdrawal of all of its capital account, a Limited Partner shall be deemed to have withdrawn from the Partnership, and upon notice of such withdrawal, a Limited Partner shall not be entitled to exercise any voting rights afforded to Limited Partners under the Partnership Agreement.

The value of the Limited Partner's capital account is determined in accordance with Section 9.01 of the Partnership Agreement, which is calculated to include original and additional capital contributions and withdrawals by a Limited Partner, and increases or decreases in the net asset value of the Partnership ("Net Asset Value") allocable to the withdrawing Limited Partner through the date of withdrawal.

Limitations on Withdrawals. The Partnership may suspend or postpone the payment of any withdrawals from capital accounts (i) in the event that Limited Partners, in the aggregate, request withdrawals of twenty-five percent (25%) or more of the value of the Partnership's capital accounts as of any date of withdrawal; (ii) during the existence of any state of affairs which, in the opinion of the General Partner, makes the disposition of the Partnership's investments impractical or prejudicial to the Partners, or where such state of affairs, in the opinion of the General Partner, makes the determination of the price or value of the Partnership's investments impractical or prejudicial to the Partners; (iii) where any withdrawals or distributions, in the opinion of the General Partner, would result in the violation of any applicable law or regulation; or (iv) for such other reasons or for such other periods as the General Partner may in good faith determine.

Required Withdrawals. The General Partner may, in its sole discretion, require a Limited Partner to withdraw any or all of the value of the Limited Partner's capital account on five (5) days notice.

Reserves. The General Partner may cause the Partnership to establish such reserves as it deems necessary for contingent Partnership liabilities, including estimated expenses in connection therewith, which could reduce the amount of a distribution upon withdrawal.

Withdrawals, Resignation, and Transfers by General Partner

The General Partner and/or its principals and affiliates may withdraw all or any of the value in their capital accounts (including any Performance Allocation (as defined below)) at any time, from time to time, without the consent of or notice to any of the Limited Partners. The General Partner may resign as the general partner of the Partnership upon thirty (30) days written notice to the Limited Partners. Upon such resignation of the sole-remaining General Partner, or upon its bankruptcy or dissolution, the remaining Limited Partners have the right to appoint a substitute general partner; otherwise the Partnership will be dissolved pursuant to the procedures set forth in the Partnership Agreement. The Partnership Agreement permits the General Partner to appoint additional general partners and to transfer its general partner interest to an affiliate of the General Partner without the consent of Limited Partners.

Performance Allocation to the General Partner

The General Partner shall receive an annual performance allocation ("Performance Allocation") at the close of each fiscal year equal to 10 percent of the portion of the Partnership's annual net income (including realized and unrealized gains and net of the Management Fee) attributable to each Limited Partner as of the close of such year. The Performance Allocation shall be (i) subject to a Loss Carryforward provision (as discussed below), and (ii) reduced, if necessary, to ensure that the Limited Partner's rate of return is at least equal to the "Hurdle Rate" for such capital account for such fiscal year. The Hurdle Rate shall equal a [ ]% annual return on a Limited Partner's capital account balance for the fiscal year (or as such rate may be adjusted for additions and withdrawals to a Limited Partner's capital account during the year to reflect the portion of the year that an investment was held). In the event that the rate of return of any Limited Partner's capital account does not exceed the Hurdle Rate in any fiscal year, such deficit shall not be carried forward as to any Limited Partner to future fiscal years.

The General Partner shall also receive the Performance Allocation upon any withdrawal by a Limited Partner, as to amounts withdrawn, whether voluntary or involuntary, and upon dissolution of the Partnership. The Performance Allocation shall be in addition to the proportionate allocations of income and profits, or losses, to the General Partner and/or its affiliates based upon their capital accounts relative to the capital accounts of all Partners. The General Partner, in its sole discretion, may waive, defer, or reduce the Performance Allocation with respect to any Limited Partner for any period of time, or agree to modify the Performance Allocation for that Limited Partner. The General Partner may, in its discretion, reallocate a portion of the Performance Allocation to certain Limited Partners.

High Water Mark The Performance Allocation is subject to what is commonly known as a "high water mark" procedure. That is, if the Partnership has a net loss in any fiscal year, this loss will be carried forward as to each Limited Partner to future fiscal years (such amount is referred to as the "Loss Carryforward"). Whenever there is a Loss Carryforward for a Limited Partner with respect to a fiscal year, the General Partner will not receive the Performance Allocation from such Limited Partner for future fiscal years until the Loss Carryforward amount for such Limited Partner has been recovered (i.e., when the Loss Carryforward amount has been exceeded by the cumulative profits allocable to such Limited Partner for the fiscal years following the Loss Carryforward). Once the Loss Carryforward has been recovered, the Performance Allocation shall be based on the excess profits (over the Loss Carryforward amount) as to each Limited Partner, rather than on all profits. The "high water mark" procedure prevents the General Partner from receiving the Performance Allocation as to profits that simply restore previous losses and is intended to ensure that the Performance Allocation is based on the long-term performance of an investment in the Partnership.

When a Limited Partner withdraws capital, any Loss Carryforward will be adjusted downward in proportion to the withdrawal. The General Partner may agree with any Limited Partner to apply a different Loss Carryforward provision for such Limited Partner.

Management Fee In consideration for provision of management and administrative services, the General Partner shall receive a management fee ("Management Fee") equal to [ ] % per month (approximately [ ]% annually) of each Limited Partner's share of the Partnership's Net Asset Value. The Management Fee shall be payable monthly in arrears and calculated as of the last day of each calendar month. A pro-rata Management Fee will be charged to Limited Partners on any amounts permitted to be invested during any calendar month. The General Partner, in its sole discretion, may waive or reduce the Management Fee with respect to one or more Limited Partners for any period of time, or agree to apply a different Management Fee for that Limited Partner.

Expenses

Organizational Expenses. The Partnership shall pay or reimburse the General Partner for all expenses related to organizing the Partnership, including, but not limited to, legal and accounting fees, printing and mailing expenses, and government filing fees (including blue sky filing fees).

Operating Expenses. The Partnership shall pay or reimburse the General Partner and its affiliates for (A) all expenses incurred in connection with the ongoing offer and sale of Interests, including, but not limited to, marketing expenses, documentation of performance, and the admission of Limited Partners, (B) all operating expenses of the Partnership such as tax preparation fees, governmental fees and taxes, administrator fees, communications with Limited Partners and ongoing legal, accounting, auditing, bookkeeping, consulting, and other professional fees and expenses, and (C) all Partnership research, due diligence, and trading costs and expenses (e.g., expenses related to the acquisition of information needed to evaluate, select, and monitor Managers and markets, related research, margin interest, expenses related to short sales, custodial fees, and clearing and settlement charges). The General Partner or its affiliates, in their sole discretion, may from time to time pay for any of the foregoing Partnership expenses or waive their right to reimbursement for any such expenses, as well as terminate any such voluntary payment or waiver of reimbursement.

General Partner's Expenses. The General Partner will pay its own general operating and overhead type expenses associated with providing the investment management and administrative services required under the Partnership Agreement.

Determination of Net Asset Value

Net Asset Value is determined in accordance with Section 9.05 of the Partnership Agreement and is generally equal to the amount by which the value of the

Partnership's assets exceeds the amount of its liabilities. Net Asset Value determinations are made by the General Partner as of the end of each month (or other period, as the case may be) in accordance with U.S. generally accepted accounting principles consistently applied (except that the General Partner intends to capitalize and amortize organizational costs over a period of sixty (60) months, from the date the Partnership commences operations, provided that such capitalization and amortization will not result in the qualification of the Partnership's financial statements). In the case of investments in underlying limited partnerships or other commingled investment vehicles that are not readily marketable, which investments are expected to constitute most of the Partnership's assets, the net asset value calculation provided by the administrators of those underlying vehicles will be used in determining the Partnership's Net Asset Value. Securities that have no public market and all other assets of the Partnership are considered at such value as the General Partner may reasonably determine in consultation with such industry professionals and other third parties as the General Partner deems appropriate. Neither the General Partner nor any of its affiliates will be responsible for calculating the net asset value of the underlying investments or for verifying the accuracy and completeness of any such values received. All values assigned to securities by the General Partner pursuant to the Partnership Agreement are final and conclusive as to all Partners.

The interest of the Partners in profits, losses, and increases and decreases in Net Asset Value shall be allocated to each Partner at the end of each month in proportion to all Partners' capital accounts as of the beginning of such month. As of the end of each fiscal year, the Performance Allocation will be debited from each Limited Partner's capital account and credited to the General Partner's capital account.

Allocation of Profit and Loss

To determine how the economic gains and losses of the Partnership will be shared, the Partnership Agreement allocates net income or loss (increases and decreases in Net Asset Value) to each Partner's capital account. Net income or net loss includes all portfolio gains and losses, whether realized or unrealized, plus all other Partnership items of income (such as interest) and less all Partnership expenses. Generally, net income or net loss for each month (or other period, as the case may be) will be allocated to the Partners in proportion to their capital account balances as of the start of such month (or such other period). Capital account balances will reflect capital contributions, previous allocations of increases and decreases in Net Asset Value, and withdrawals.

Allocation of Taxable Income and Loss

For income tax purposes, all items of taxable income, gain, loss, deduction, and credit will be allocated among the Partners at the end of each fiscal year in a manner consistent with their economic interests in the Partnership. In light of the fact that the Partnership does not intend to make distributions, to the extent the Partnership's investment activities are successful, Limited Partners should expect to receive allocations of income and loss, and may incur tax liabilities from an investment in the Partnership without receiving cash distributions from the Partnership with which to pay those liabilities. To obtain cash from the Partnership to pay taxes, if any, Limited Partners may be required to make withdrawals, subject to the limitations herein.

In the event a Limited Partner withdraws all of its capital account from the Partnership, the General Partner, in its sole discretion, may make a special allocation to the Limited Partner for income tax purposes of the net capital gains recognized by the Partnership, in the last year in which the withdrawing Limited Partner participated in the performance of the Partnership, in such manner as will reduce the amount, if any, by which such Limited Partner's capital account exceeds its income tax basis in its interest in the Partnership before such allocation.

New Issues

From time to time, the Partnership or underlying Managers may purchase securities that are part of a public distribution. Under rules adopted by the National Association of Securities Dealers, Inc. ("NASD"), certain persons engaged in the securities, banking, or financial services industries (and members of their family) (collectively, "Restricted Persons") are restricted from participating in initial public offerings of equity securities ("New Issues"), subject to a de minimis exemption. Participation in New Issues shall be limited to (i) those Limited Partners who are not Restricted Persons, and (ii) those Limited Partners who are Restricted Persons but only to the extent that such participation by Restricted Persons does not exceed levels permitted under applicable NASD rules. The General Partner shall be entitled to receive the Performance Allocation with respect to any profits in the New Issues Account.

The income or loss of a New Issue purchased directly by the Partnership shall be accounted for separately until the first to occur of (A) its sale, or (B) the close of trading on the first day that the security may be publicly traded. Upon disposition, any profits or losses resulting from securities transactions in the new issues account in any fiscal period will be credited or debited to the capital accounts of Limited Partners participating in New Issues in accordance with their interests therein.

The returns to Limited Partners on their investments in the Partnership may differ depending upon whether they are a Restricted Person. In the event the NASD adopts amendments to its New Issue rules, the General Partner is authorized to amend the Partnership Agreement without the consent of the Limited Partners to conform to such amendments.

Reports to Limited Partners

Each Limited Partner will receive the following: (i) annual financial statements of the Partnership audited by an independent certified public accounting firm, (ii) at the discretion of the General Partner, a monthly letter from the General Partner discussing the results of the Partnership, (iii) copies of such Limited Partner's Schedule K-1 to the Partnership's tax returns, and (iv) other reports as determined by the General Partner in its sole discretion. The Partnership shall bear all fees incurred in providing such tax returns and reports.

The General Partner may agree to provide certain Limited Partners with additional information on the underlying investments of the Partnership, as well as access to the General Partner and their employees for relevant information.

Transferability of Interests

As a Limited Partner, you may not assign or transfer your Interest (except by operation of law) without the consent of the General Partner, which consent may be given or withheld in its sole discretion. No transfer of an Interest by a Limited Partner will be permitted if it would result in termination of the Partnership for federal income tax purposes. Transfers of Interests are subject to other restrictions set forth in the Partnership Agreement, including compliance with federal and state securities laws.

Due to these limitations on transferability, Limited Partners may be required to hold their Interests indefinitely unless they withdraw from the Partnership in accordance with the procedures set forth in the Partnership Agreement.

Distributions

The Partnership does not expect to make any distributions to Limited Partners from profits or capital, except pursuant to requests for withdrawals and upon termination of the Partnership.

Upon the termination of the Partnership (as further described in Article [ ] of the Partnership Agreement), the assets of the Partnership will be liquidated (or distributed), and the proceeds of liquidation will be used to pay off known liabilities, establish reserves for contingent liabilities and expenses of liquidation, and any remaining balance will be applied and distributed in proportion to the respective capital accounts of the Partners.

Voting Rights and Amendments

The voting rights of Limited Partners are very limited. Other than as explicitly set forth in the Partnership Agreement, Limited Partners have no voting rights as to the Partnership or its management. Generally, the Partnership Agreement may be amended only with the consent of the General Partner and Limited Partners owning more than fifty percent (50%) in Interests, except that the General Partner may amend the Partnership Agreement without the consent of or notice to any of the Limited Partners if, in the opinion of the General Partner, the amendment does not materially adversely affect any Limited Partner.

Bank Holding Companies

Limited Partners that are Bank Holding Companies ("BHC Limited Partners"), as defined by Section 2(a) of the Bank Holding Company Act of 1956, as amended ("BHCA"), are limited to 4.99% of the voting interest in the Partnership under Section 4(c)(6) of the BHCA. The portion of interest in the Partnership held by a BHC Limited Partner in excess of 4.99% of the total outstanding aggregate voting interests of all Limited Partners shall be deemed non-voting interests in the Partnership. BHC Limited Partners holding non-voting interests in the Partnership are permitted to vote (i) on any proposal to dissolve or continue the business of the Partnership under the Partnership Agreement and (ii) on matters with respect to which voting rights are not considered to be "voting securities" under 12 C.F.R. § 225.2(q)(2), including such matters that may "significantly and adversely" affect a BHC Limited Partner (such as amendments to the Partnership Agreement or modifications of the terms of its interest). Except with regard to restrictions on voting, non-voting interests are identical to all other interests held by Limited Partners.

Liability of Limited Partners

A Limited Partner's liability to the Partnership is limited to the amount of such Limited Partner's Capital Account, including the amount it has contributed to the capital of the Partnership. Once an Interest has been paid for in full, the holder of that Interest will have no further obligation at any time to make any loans or additional capital contributions to the Partnership. No Limited Partner shall be personally liable for any debts or obligations of the Partnership. Under Delaware law, when a Limited Partner receives a return of all or any part of such Limited Partner's capital contribution, the Limited Partner may be liable to the Partnership for any sum, not in excess of such return of capital (together with interest), if at the time of such distribution the Limited Partner knew that the Partnership was prohibited from making such distribution pursuant to the Partnership Act.

Other Activities of General Partner and Affiliates	Neither the General Partner nor [ ] is required to manage the Partnership as their sole and exclusive function. They may engage in other business activities including competing ventures and/or other unrelated employment. In addition to managing the Partnership's investments, the General Partner [ ] and their affiliates may provide investment advice to other parties and may manage other accounts and/or establish other private investment funds in the future that employ an investment strategy similar to that of the Partnership. See "MANAGEMENT."
Exculpation and Indemnification	The General Partner will be generally liable to third parties for all obligations of the Partnership to the extent such obligations are not paid by the Partnership or are not by their terms limited to recourse against specific assets. The General Partner shall not be liable to the Partnership or the Limited Partners for any action or inaction in connection with the business of the Partnership unless such action or inaction is found to constitute gross negligence or willful misconduct. The Partnership (but not the Limited Partners individually) is obligated to indemnify the General Partner and its managers and members from any claim, loss, damage, or expense incurred by such persons relating to the business of the Partnership, provided that such indemnity will not extend to conduct determined by a final, non-appealable court of competent jurisdiction to constitute gross negligence or willful misconduct.
Term	The term of the Partnership shall continue indefinitely until terminated in accordance with the Partnership Agreement. Under the Partnership Agreement, the Partnership may be terminated at the election of the General Partner.
Fiscal Year	The fiscal year of the Partnership shall end on December 31 of each year, which fiscal year may be changed by the General Partner, in its sole and absolute discretion.
Attorneys	Sadis & Goldberg LLP, New York, New York, acts as legal counsel to the General Partner and the Partnership in connection with the offering of Interests and other ongoing matters and does not represent the Limited Partners.

Auditors	[ ], acts as the auditors of the Partnership.
Administrator	[ ], acts as the administrator of the Partnership.
Address for Inquiries	You are invited to, and it is highly recommended that you do, meet with the General Partner for a further explanation of the terms and conditions of this offering of Interests and to obtain any additional information necessary to verify the information contained in this Memorandum, to the extent the General Partner possesses such information or can acquire it without unreasonable effort or expense. Requests for such information should be directed to: [ ].

Management

Role of the General Partner

The General Partner of the Partnership, [ ], a Delaware limited liability company and investment adviser registered with the State of [ ], commenced operations in October 2004. The General Partner is solely responsible for researching, selecting, and monitoring investments by the Partnership and making decisions on when and how much to invest with or withdraw from a particular investment. Limited Partners do not have any right to participate in the management of the Partnership and have limited voting rights.

As the managing member and controlling person of the General Partner, [ ] controls all of the Partnership's operations and activities, including the management of its portfolio.

The General Partner employs certain administrative personnel and may employ additional personnel in the future, terminate existing personnel, or change the roles, title, or function of existing personnel at any time without further notice to Limited Partners. No material administrative, civil, or criminal actions have ever been brought against the Partnership, the General Partner, and their affiliates, or [ ].

Other Activities of General Partner and Affiliates

The General Partner is not required to manage the Partnership as its sole and exclusive function. The General Partner may engage in other business activities and is only required to devote such time to the Partnership as it deems necessary to accomplish the purposes of the Partnership. Similarly, although [ ] expects to devote a significant amount of his time to the business of the General Partner and the Partnership, he is only required to devote so much of his time to these entities as he determines in his sole discretion.

In addition to managing the Partnership's investments, the General Partner, [ ], and their affiliates may choose to provide investment management and other services to other parties and may manage other accounts and/or establish other private investment funds in the future (both domestic and offshore) that employ an investment strategy similar to that of the Partnership.

Appendix C

Example of Material Included in a Cayman-Based Fund for Tax-Exempt US-Investors

The material for this section of the book has been supplied by Ingrid Pierce, partner head of the hedge fund practice at the Cayman Island–based law firm Walkers.

Part 1: Establishing an Offshore Fund Domiciled in the Cayman Islands[1]

Fund Structure

The choice of fund structure will be driven by the target investor base, investment management requirements, and tax structuring concerns.

[1]For information about the legal and regulatory requirements for establishing offshore funds in the British Virgin Islands or Jersey, contact the authors of this guide

Funds may be established as exempted companies, exempted limited partnerships, or exempted trusts.

Exempted company An exempted company must have a registered office in the Cayman Islands and keep registers of its directors and any security interests granted by the company at its registered office. It must also maintain a register of shareholders (although this need not be maintained in the Cayman Islands). Shareholders of an exempted company incorporated with limited liability will have limited liability, usually limited to the amount, if any, unpaid on their shares.

Segregated portfolio company An exempted company may be registered as an exempted segregated portfolio company ("**SPC**"). Segregated portfolios of an SPC may be established with the benefit of statutory segregation of their respective assets and liabilities.

Exempted limited partnership An exempted limited partnership must have at least one limited partner and at least one general partner. At least one general partner must be a resident in the Cayman Islands (if an individual), be registered under the Companies Law (if a company), be registered as a foreign company under the Companies Law (if a foreign company), or be an exempted limited partnership itself.

A limited partner of an exempted limited partnership will not be liable for the debts and obligations of the exempted limited partnership except (i) as expressly set out in the partnership agreement, (ii) if such limited partner becomes involved in the conduct or management of that exempted limited partnership's business, or (iii) if such limited partner is obliged pursuant to Cayman law to return a payment deemed received and representing any part of its contribution within six months before an insolvency of the exempted limited partnership.

A Cayman exempted limited partnership does not have separate legal personality. An exempted limited partnership, however, has some features that are synonymous with limited partnerships with separate legal personality. A Cayman exempted limited partnership can hold property in its own name, and such partnerships can be stacked on top of each other.

The general partner must maintain a register of limited partnership interests and forward a copy to the fund's registered office in the Cayman Islands within 21 business days of any changes thereto.

Exempted trust An exempted trust must be established by a trustee. The trustee is usually a licensed Cayman Islands trust company although a non–Cayman Islands trustee may be appointed. Unless otherwise agreed with a unitholder, unitholders of an exempted trust will have limited liability, usually limited to the amount, if any, unpaid on their units.

Capital structure

An open-ended corporate or unit trust hedge fund will generally either:

(1) issue shares or units with voting rights to all investors; or

(2) issue: (a) management shares or units with voting rights (with or without any economic participation in the fund) to be held (i) by or on behalf of the promoter or (ii) by a trustee under a dedicated trust arrangement such as a Cayman Islands STAR trust and (b) redeemable participating shares or units with economic rights, but without any, or with limited, voting rights, to be held by investors.

An investor in an open-ended exempted limited partnership will hold a partnership interest as a limited partner. The partnership agreement will set out the extent of a limited partner's economic rights and any voting rights (which may include the right to vote on certain amendments to the partnership agreement).

Regulation

This guide assumes that the fund will be regulated by the Cayman Islands Monetary Authority ("CIMA") under the Mutual Funds Law (as amended) of the Cayman Islands (the "Mutual Funds Law").

The Mutual Funds Law defines a "mutual fund" as "a company, unit trust, or partnership that issues equity interests, the purpose or effect of which is the pooling of investor funds with the aim of spreading investment risks and enabling investors in the mutual fund to receive profits or gains from the acquisition, holding, management, or disposal of investments…" For these purposes an "equity interest" is defined as "a share, trust unit, or partnership interest that (a) carries an entitlement to participate in the profits or gains of the company, unit trust, or partnership and (b) is redeemable or repurchasable at the option of the investor… before the commencement of winding up or dissolution of the company… but does not include debt."

There are three categories of regulated mutual funds in the Cayman Islands:

Licensed Funds Licensed mutual funds are funds that hold a license under the Mutual Funds Law. They must have either a registered office in the Cayman Islands or, if a unit trust, a trustee that is licensed under the Banks and Trust

Companies Law (as amended) of the Cayman Islands and are subject to a prior approval process, requiring CIMA to be satisfied with the experience and reputation of the promoter and administrator and that the business of the fund and the offering of its interests will be carried out in a proper way.

Funds with no minimum investment threshold Mutual funds with a minimum subscription level of less than US$100,000.00 must have a licensed mutual fund administrator providing their principal office in the Cayman Islands.

Funds with a $100,000 (U.S.) minimum investment threshold Mutual funds where either: (i) the minimum equity interest purchasable by a prospective investor is $100,000 (U.S.) or equivalent; or (ii) the equity interests are listed on an approved stock exchange or over the counter market, have the fewest regulatory burdens in the Cayman Islands. Such funds must file an offering document, appoint an administrator (whether inside or outside of the Cayman Islands), and must have their accounts audited annually by an approved Cayman Islands auditor. Funds falling into this category constitute the vast majority of hedge funds established in the Cayman Islands and it is likely that any hedge fund with a sophisticated investor base will be established this way. No approval from CIMA is required prior to launch of such a fund.

Checklist: key steps[2]

- Confirm the proposed name of the fund is available
- Confirm the registered office of the fund in the Cayman Islands and enter into Registered Office Services Agreement (if any)
- Form the entity and obtain the certificate of incorporation
- Appoint the directors[3] and officers (if any)
- Confirm the authorized share capital and capital structure
- Prepare any amended memorandum and articles of association[4]
- Apply for Undertaking, pursuant to the Tax Concessions Law (as amended) of the Cayman Islands

[2]For the purposes of this checklist we have assumed the fund will be established as an exempted limited company.

[3]A regulated mutual fund must have at least two directors.

[4]If the share capital is to be restructured or other amendments are required to the memorandum and articles, director and shareholder resolutions will be required to adopt the amended and restated memorandum and articles.

- Prepare the key documents and agreements:
  - Offering document and any supplements thereto
  - Subscription documents
  - Investment management agreement
  - Sub-advisory agreement (if any)
  - Administration agreement
  - Custodian agreement
  - Prime brokerage agreement
  - Lending / security agreements
  - Other agreements as applicable (e.g. placement agreement, distribution agreement, listing documents if the fund is to be listed, charge entries)
  - Director services agreements (if any)

Obtain letter of consent from the auditor confirming its appointment and the financial year of the fund.

Obtain letter of consent from the administrator confirming its appointment and listing administration services to be provided. Typically one administrator is appointed, but if the administrator provides registrar and transfer agency services and another agent provides the NAV calculation, consent letters will be required from each person.

Prepare mutual fund registration form (commonly a Form MF1) Hold a meeting of the board prior to launch to approve the offering. The resolutions will usually document the board's approval of the offering document, the issue of offered shares, the appointment of service providers and attorneys, the agreements to be entered into by the fund, the mutual fund registration form, and the means by which the fund will comply with anti-money laundering regulations.

Documents to be filed with CIMA upon launch

- Offering document and any supplements thereto
- Certified copy of the certificate of incorporation
- Executed Mutual Fund registration form
- Executed auditor's consent letter
- Executed administrator's consent letter(s)

The Offering Document Under Cayman Islands law, an offering document must describe the equity interests being offered in all material respects and must contain such other information as is necessary to enable a prospective investor to make an informed decision as to whether or not to subscribe for or purchase equity interests in the fund.

The form of the offering document below is an abbreviated summary highlighting the key issues to be considered when launching an offshore fund.

Part 2: Summary of Key Disclosures for Cayman Islands Offering Document[5]

LEGEND

Describe any restrictions on the offering in all jurisdictions in which the fund may be offered. Note that no member of the public in the Cayman Islands may subscribe for any shares in the fund.

DIRECTORY

The directory should list the name and address of the registered office of the fund and all key service providers, including U.S. and Cayman Islands counsel.

If the offering document contains an abbreviated summary of terms, the summary should be qualified by more detailed information contained elsewhere in the offering document, the articles of association of the fund, and in other documents relating to the fund referred to in the offering document.

THE FUND

Describe the fund and the capital structure.

If the fund will invest all or substantially all of its assets through a "master-feeder" fund structure, describe the structure and the master fund. If other feeder funds (whether onshore or offshore funds) have been established to invest in the master fund, they should be disclosed. Disclose whether other investment vehicles may be formed in the future to invest in the master fund.

INVESTMENT OBJECTIVE, STRATEGY, AND POLICY

This section will contain a detailed description of the investment objectives, strategy, and policy of the fund, including any investment restrictions.

[5]For the purposes of this summary we have assumed that the fund will be established as an exempted limited company.

THE OFFERING

Describe the shares or classes of participating shares being offered and whether they will carry the right to vote or have limited or no voting rights.

Disclose the classes of shares being offered (participating redeemable shares, and the rights and restrictions of each class (e.g. different liquidity, fees etc.).

Do the directors have discretion to issue additional classes, sub-classes, or series of participating shares on different terms?

Eligible Investors Describe persons who may invest in the fund and any restrictions on eligibility.

Minimum investment What is the minimum initial investment, and can this be reduced in the discretion of the directors? Note that the majority of funds have a minimum initial investment of $100,000 (U.S.).

Is there a minimum subsequent investment amount? Can this be waived / reduced? Is there a minimum holding investors must maintain?

Subscriptions Disclose the subscription policy and key terms. What is the subscription price per share for initial and subsequent subscriptions?

Explain the dates and times by which subscription forms and subscription monies must be received and by whom. Describe the rights of the directors / administrator / others to reject subscriptions, including for inadequate due diligence or anti–money laundering compliance. Will share certificates be issued? In what circumstances can shares be transferred, and whose consent is required?

Disclose the person who maintains the fund's register of shareholders.

Redemptions Set out in detail all relevant redemption terms including the number of days prior written notice required for a redemption prior to the relevant redemption date, the form (if any) of such notice, and the manner in which the redemption price will be determined.

Disclose any restrictions on redemptions, including any lock up (hard or soft including any redemption fees), any gate provisions (stacked gate or investor-level gate), any holdbacks (what percentage and for how long), and whether any interest will be payable on any final payment of redemption proceeds. Does the fund have power to clawback redemption proceeds? In what circumstances?

Disclose whether the fund has power to pay some or all of the redemption proceeds in kind. Consider disclosing the nature of any such redemptions and whether the fund or the investment manager will be responsible for selecting the investments to be delivered in kind.

Can the fund waive any or all of the redemption restrictions?

Does the fund have power to create side pockets and in what circumstances? Must the asset be illiquid or hard to value on acquisition, or can the investment manager determine to place assets that subsequently become illiquid into a side pocket? Are there any restrictions on the percentage of the fund's assets that may be held in the side pocket? In what circumstances will the investments in the side pocket be realized or deemed realized? Disclose the mechanics of the side pocket and relevant valuation issues.

In what circumstances can the fund compulsorily redeem some or all of a shareholder's shares?

Suspensions Disclose the circumstances in which the fund may suspend the calculation of the net asset value and / or the subscription and / or voluntary redemption of shares and / or the right to receive the redemption proceeds. Are the directors required to consult with the investment manager prior to the imposition of a suspension?

Disclose the status of redemption requests that are pending upon imposition of a suspension. Can they be withdrawn? Whose consent (if any) is required? When will shareholders be notified of the suspension and its termination? In what order will redemption proceeds be paid following termination of the suspension?

REPORTS TO SHAREHOLDERS

In addition to the annual audited financial statements, describe any other reports to be provided for example net asset value statements or other unaudited performance reports and the frequency of such reporting.

INVESTMENT MANAGER

Describe the investment manager of the fund. Will the investment manager assume responsibility for all investment decisions or delegate to a sub-investment manager or advisor?

Describe the obligations and duties of the Investment Manager and key terms of the investment management agreement, including fees, termination provisions, and indemnities.

Describe the management fee applicable to each class.

Describe the performance fee applicable to each class. Which method of calculation is used: series accounting or equalization? Is there a hurdle rate?

Disclose biographical information on the principals of the investment manager and a description of their role or duties.

Information on the Directors, Administrator, and Other Service Providers

The Directors List the directors and disclose their biographies. Disclose the manner in which a director may be appointed or removed. Disclose limits of liability and nature of indemnity available to directors.

The Administrator Describe the administrator and key terms of the administration agreement, including fees, termination provisions, and indemnities. Assuming the administrator is responsible for maintaining the register of shareholders, this should be noted. The register should include both participating and management shares. The administrator is usually responsible for undertaking anti–money laundering verification on behalf of a fund and, if so, this should be noted.

Other service providers Describe the other service providers (for example custodian, prime broker) and key terms of each agreement, including fees, termination provisions, and indemnities. Note in particular any limitation on liability and the scope of any indemnity to the provider and / or its affiliates.

The Auditor Disclose the auditor/s appointed[6], the fund's financial year-end, the period covered by the first audit, and the date on which audited financial statements will be provided to investors.

EXPENSES

In addition to service provider fees, disclose any other fees and expenses borne by the Fund.

Will establishment expenses be amortized over a longer period than stipulated by the fund's adopted accounting standards?

DETERMINATION OF NET ASSET VALUE

Disclose the method of determination of net asset value per share and per class and the accounting principles to be applied.

Disclose how different types of securities will be valued and the party responsible for valuation. Is the administrator responsible for calculating the net asset value or will it independently price the securities? If not, disclose who is responsible for pricing the securities. If the investment manager is involved in determining the value of any security, does it have discretion to assign values other than in accordance with the stated valuation policy? In what circumstances?

[6]Note the Cayman Islands Monetary Authority requirement for regulated funds to have an approved auditor filing the audited financial statements and fund annual return.

RISK FACTORS

The offering document will invariably contain a buyer beware statement to the effect that an investment in the fund involves significant risks and is suitable only for those persons who can bear the economic risk of the loss of their entire investment and who have limited need for liquidity in their investment. There is usually a statement that no assurance can be made that the fund will achieve its investment objective.

A comprehensive list of risk factors relating to underlying securities should be disclosed. This might include lack of operating history, dependence on key individuals, absence of regulatory oversight, liquidity risk, market risk, investment and trading risks, counterparty risk, cross-class liability risk, and structural risk (e.g. if investing through a master-feeder structure).

If the fund may enter into side letters with certain investors, describe the nature of the additional and/or different rights that may be granted to such investors and consider the risks to other investors of the grant of such rights.

CONFLICTS OF INTEREST

Material conflicts of interest must be disclosed. These might include conflicts relating to the directors, principals of the investment manager, or other service providers, including affiliates.

TAX CONSIDERATIONS

Disclose relevant U.S. tax disclosure and Cayman Islands tax disclosure. Specify whether the fund has applied for or has received an undertaking from the Governor in Cabinet of the Cayman Islands to the effect that, for a certain period (up to 30 years) from such date, no law that thereafter is enacted in the Cayman Islands imposing any tax or duty to be levied on profits, income, or on gains or appreciation, or any tax in the nature of estate duty or inheritance tax, will apply to any property comprised in or any income arising under the fund, or to the shareholders thereof, in respect of any such property or income.

ANTI–MONEY LAUNDERING

Disclose applicable U.S. anti–money laundering regulations and requirements.

Describe the fund's responsibility for the prevention of money laundering and provide detailed disclosure of the requirements under the Proceeds of Crime Law and the Money Laundering Regulations (as amended) of the Cayman Islands.

CAYMAN ISLANDS MUTUAL FUNDS LAW

If the fund falls within the definition of a "mutual fund" under the Mutual Funds Law (as amended) of the Cayman Islands, include appropriate disclosure of the fund's regulation under such Law by the Cayman Islands Monetary Authority ("CIMA") and disclose the key filing requirements. Describe CIMA's powers with respect to regulated funds in the event of non-compliance with the Mutual Funds Law.

Glossary

absolute-return fund an absolute return fund attempts to perform positively for investors regardless of general direction or market conditions by investing in a range of long and short positions with low correlation to the markets. An absolute-return fund measures the gain or loss of the portfolio as a percentage of capital invested.

ABX also known as the asset-backed securities index, is a credit derivative with asset-backed securities underlying it.

accredited investor rule 501 or Regulation D of the Securities Act of 1933 defines an accredited investor as any of the following:

- A bank, insurance company, registered investment company, business development company, or small business investment company.
- An employee benefit plan, within the meaning of the Employee Retirement Income Security Act, if a bank, insurance company, or registered investment adviser makes the investment decisions, or if the plan has total assets in excess of $5 million.
- A charitable organization, corporation, or partnership with assets exceeding $5 million.
- A director, executive officer, or general partner of the company selling the securities.
- A business in which all the equity owners are accredited investors.
- A natural person who has individual net worth, or joint net worth with the person's spouse, that exceeds $1 million at the time of purchase.
- A natural person with income exceeding $200,000 in each of the two most recent years or joint income with a spouse exceeding $300,000 for those years and a reasonable expectation of the same income level in the current year.
- A trust with assets in excess of $5 million, not formed to acquire the securities offered, whose purchases a sophisticated person makes.

administrator a service provider hired by an investment manager to calculate performance and net asset value for the fund, perform record-keeping functions, perform fund accounting, act as transfer agent, and maintain all books and records for the fund manager.

alpha the premium investment return of an investment over a benchmark index such as the S&P 500. Positive alpha indicates that the investment manager has earned a premium over the index and returns are driven by the manager, not the index. The stronger the investment results relative to the index, the stronger the management team of the investor.

alternative assets include any non-traditional investments that would not be found in the standard investment portfolio. Alternative assets include hedge funds, private equity funds, real estate partnerships, forestry investments, and oil and gas partnerships.

arbitrage an investment strategy that attempts to exploit the price difference between the same or similar financial instruments, commodities, or currencies. An arbitrageur may buy a contract for crude oil in the New York market at a lower price and simultaneously sell it in the Chicago market at a higher price.

assets under management assets under management (AUM) includes all investments, leveraged and unleveraged, including cash, that are managed by a fund manager.

average annual return (annualized rate of return) cumulative compounded gains and losses divided by the number of years of a fund's existence.

average rate of return sometimes referred to as rate of return, or ROR, the average return of investment over a fixed period of time. ROR is used to compare returns on investments over a period of time, and is usually expressed on an annualized basis.

back-test back testing uses historical data to evaluate past performance results. Often referred to as a hypothetical portfolio, it simulates investment returns over a past period of time to determine the performance outcome if the strategy had been followed in the past.

basis points one basis point is 1/100th of a percentage point or 0.01 percent. Conversely, 100 basis points (bps) is 1 percent.

bear market a market that is characterized by a period of falling prices that may last from several months to several years.

beta the measure of volatility or risk of a security or portfolio in comparison to an index. Beta represents the percentage change in the price given a 1 percent change of the index. The higher the beta, the higher the risk. A beta of 1.0 indicates that the asset follows the index while a beta less than 1.0 indicates that the asset has lower volatility.

black box a computer program where a series of inputs are processed utilizing pre-programmed logical procedures in order to return an output. This output is then used by traders to determine whether to buy, sell, or hold a security. A black box is an integral part of any quantitative strategy fund.

bloomberg terminal a software and hardware system that enables its users to view and analyze market data movements and securities trades in real time.

bull market a market that is characterized by a period of rising prices that may last from several months to several years.

CAGR compounded average growth rate is the year-after-year growth of an investment for a specified period of time.

calmar ratio used to determine return on a downside risk-adjusted basis and it can be computed by dividing the compounded annual return by the maximum drawdown (see *Drawdown*).

cap-and-trade a cap-and-trade system is a means to provide economic incentives for firms to reduce emissions by allowing their reductions to be converted to and traded as credits in given emissions markets.

capital structure arbitrage consists of investors profiting from a pricing inefficiency within the capital structure of a single firm. For example, an investor can go long convertible bonds and short the underlying common stock.

carbon emissions trading an example of a cap-and-trade system particular to carbon dioxide emissions.

clearing the process of reconciling transactions between a fund manager and broker dealers and prime broker after trades are entered and executed and settled.

collateralized bond obligations (CBO) are an example of a structured credit product backed by fixed income assets placed into separate tranches, with corresponding credit ratings: senior tranches, mezzanine tranches, and equity tranches. Losses flow upstream from the junior tranches onto the senior tranches and, therefore, the riskier lower tranches offer higher coupon rates (see *Coupon rate*).

collateralized debt obligations (CDO) are an example of a structured credit product backed by fixed income assets placed into separate tranches, with corresponding credit ratings: senior tranches, mezzanine tranches, and equity tranches. Losses flow upstream from the junior tranches onto the senior tranches and therefore, the riskier lower tranches offer higher coupon rates (see *Coupon rate*).

collateralized loan obligations (CLO) are similar to collateralized debt obligations (see *CDO*) with the difference that, in the case of CLOs, only loans are packaged into the security.

commodity trading advisor (CTA) a person or entity that provides expert advice to investors on investments in commodity futures, options, and foreign-exchange contracts is referred to as a CTA.

coupon rate the term used to describe the interest rate on a bond when it is issued. The name originates from the fact that some bonds have actual coupons attached to them that can be removed and used for redemption of payments.

credit crunch a credit crunch is an abrupt reduction of the availability of loans or the sharp increase in the cost of loans.

credit default swap index (CDX) a credit derivative that represents a basket of credit securities pertaining to various credit entities. The CDX index contains only companies from emerging markets and North America.

credit default swaps a credit derivative that involves two counterparties; party A makes periodic payments to party B and, in exchange, party A has the promise that if a third party, party C, defaults, party A will receive the full payoff from party B. Therefore, party A is said to be the buyer of credit protection, and party B is the seller of credit protection. Party C is referred to as the reference entity. Credit default swaps are used to hedge credit risks when making loans.

custodian a bank, trust company, or other financial institution that holds the fund assets and provides other services that include receiving funds from investors, distributing redemption proceeds, and providing safekeeping services and reporting fund transfers.

delta the ratio that illustrates how the change in the price of an asset affects the price of an option. For example, if a call option has a delta of 0.5, an increase of $1 in the price of the asset will result in an increase of $0.50 in the price of an option. Conversely, for a put option, a delta of 0.5 followed by an increase in price of the asset of $1 would result in a decrease in the price of the option of $0.50.

derivatives a derivative is a financial instrument that is valued based upon the underlying value of another security or benchmark index. Derivatives include options, credit default swaps, futures, interest rate swaps, and interest rate caps and floors.

diversification a portfolio strategy that is structured to lower portfolio volatility and reduce exposure by adding investments that reduces the upside and downside volatility.

drawdown the amount of decline from the prior peak return level of the fund.

due diligence due diligence is a process that describes the research of a manager and strategy by an investor that involves the performance results and operational procedures of an investment partnership and investment team. While the term originated by broker/dealers for business transactions, it refers to the overall detailed review of a hedge fund strategy and activity to ensure that the fund manager complies with the marketing documents and legal documents governing the fund and strategy.

emerging markets the term refers to emerging economies in countries that are developing and becoming mature. It refers to developing economies including Russia, Mexico, Brazil (and Latin America), India, China, much of Southeast Asia, and Eastern Europe.

enterprise risk the risk associated with the creation and management of young businesses and their transition from startups to more mature companies.

equity market neutral an expression used to describe a strategy that is free from any market risk in the equity markets to which it could have exposure.

exposure the extent to which an investment has the potential to change based on changes in market conditions. In hedge funds, exposure is measured on a net basis. Net exposure takes into account the difference between the long positions versus the short positions. For example, if a fund is 150 percent long and 65 percent short, the net exposure would be 85 percent. Gross exposure takes into consideration the total exposure, such as 215 percent gross in the above example.

event driven a type of strategy in which the manager invests in stocks of companies that are in special situations, such as in distress, in the process of being acquired, or in the constant scrutiny of the media.

fair value the price a security would trade between parties.

forward contract a forward contract is an agreement in an over-the-counter derivative instrument that requires one party to sell and another party to buy a specific security or commodity at a preset price on an agreed-upon date in the future. The forward price of the contract is contrasted with the spot price, which is the price of the asset at the spot date.

fund of funds an investment fund that implements an investment strategy that invests in other hedge funds or other investment vehicles to provide portfolio diversification for a wide range of investors. Generally, a fund of funds does not own securities directly.

futures contract an agreement to buy or sell a specific amount of commodity or security at a specific date in the future.

gamma measures the rate of change of delta with respect to the price of the underlying asset.

general partner the general partner is one or more individuals or a firm that operates, develops, and runs a limited partnership and is responsible for the debts of the partnership.

haircut a percentage that is subtracted from the value of an asset used as collateral in order to reflect the perceived risk associated with holding the asset.

high-water mark a reference in the offering documents that provides for the manager to earn an incentive fee only after the fund's performance surpasses its highest net asset value from the prior period.

hurdle rate a minimum rate of return that the fund must achieve before the fund manager receives an incentive (performance) fee. The hurdle rate may be a fixed rate such as LIBOR or the one-year Treasury bill rate plus a fixed spread of basis points.

incentive fee (performance fee) a fee that a fund manager receives that is dependent upon profits generated in the portfolio. The compensation fee is generally 20 percent of all profits over a fixed level.

inception date the specific period on which a fund begins trading.

infovest 21 a news company dedicated to covering the alternative assets industry.

IRR the annualized compounded rate of return that an investment could potentially earn, based on past performance.

leverage the amplification of results, either negative or positive, through the usage of borrowed funds or debt creation.

limited liability company (LLC) a legal structure often used by investment partnerships in which the owners of the LLC receive limited personal liability for operating the business.

limited partnership a business organizational structure in which the general partner manages the business, assumes the legal obligations for limited partners, and receives the economic benefit of the business for the benefit of the limited partners who receive the cash flow but have no corporate or legal obligations.

liquidity the ability in which an investment can be sold or converted to cash without dramatically impacting its price in the market. Liquidity will vary according to market conditions, size of the position, and historic trading volume of the security.

lockup the term that an investor must maintain an investment in the fund until the first period for redemption is permitted. Initial lockups generally are one year but may range as long as five years for some specific purpose hedge funds.

long position a position of an investor who buys a security (or derivative) and expects the value of the security to rise in price.

management fee the fee that investment partnership investors pay to the investment manager to offset the operating expenses of the underlying fund. The annual fee generally ranges from 1 percent to 2 percent of the investor's capital account balance in the fund and is usually collected on a quarterly basis.

margin call the order from a broker dealer for an investor that is using margin in a securities account to provide additional monies or securities to bring the account up to the minimum maintenance level required by the lending firm is a margin call. It also may be called a house call or maintenance call.

market neutral a strategy that seeks to reduce risk exposure to the market index. Also referred to as zero beta, the strategy seeks to achieve a return that is a spread to an index, such as Libor, by hedging long positions and will have no correlation to the underlying index. This term is often misused as the strategy should be long and short equal levels of market capitalization, sectors, and industry positions to be judged market neutral for an equity strategy.

mean-reversion a method for investing in stocks where the mean price of which a stock is traded is calculated. The investors then either purchase additional stocks when they are priced below the mean price or sell stocks when they are priced above the mean price.

minimum investment the smallest amount that an investor is permitted to invest in a hedge fund as an initial investment. Minimum investment requirements generally range from $500,000 to $5 million.

net asset value (NAV) the market value of a fund's total assets.

net exposure the percentage of a portfolio's assets invested in long positions minus the percentage of a portfolio's assets invested in short positions. For example, if a portfolio is 80 percent long and 40 percent short, net exposure will equal 40 percent (80-40).

offshore fund a private investment company open to a limited range of accredited investors that is set up outside of the United States, generally in an offshore financial center such as the Cayman Islands. It is available for investment to non-U.S. citizens or non-U.S taxpayer entities such as foundations and endowments. These offshore domiciles offer significant tax benefits for eligible investors.

onshore fund a private investment partnership that is open to a limited range of accredited investors set up in the United States. Available for investment to U.S. citizens only.

operational risk the risk associated with a company's operations. It is not inherent in either financing risk (see *Financing risk*) or systemic risk (see *Systemic risk*). It can be thought of as the risk associated with a business failing due to human incompetence.

option a contract that gives parties the right to buy or sell a specific asset or security at a specific strike price at a specific future date.

performance fee this is a fee paid to the investment manager that is based upon the increase in net asset value of the underlying fund. Performance fees are generally 20 percent of the increase of NAV and assessed on an annual basis.

PerTrac a commercially available service that provides a platform for portfolio analytics for hedge fund and traditional long-only investment.

poison pill this refers to a strategy used to increase the likelihood of negative results for an investor attempting a takeover of a company.

portfolio risk the overall risk presented by the securities in which a portfolio's assets are invested in.

prime broker prime broker refers to the full range of investment services provided by an investment bank or commercial bank to hedge funds. It includes operational services, trading, reporting, securities lending, technology support, and financing.

private-equity fund a pooled fixed life investment vehicle that makes equity or debt investments in companies with a management fee and carried interest paid to the management company.

private placement memorandum (PPM) this document sets forth the offering term for the fund and includes all business terms such as fees, restrictions, and a detailed description of the investment strategy.

pro-forma pro-forma (from the Latin "for the sake of form") is a method of describing projected figures for a current or future investment. It is important to remember that pro-forma figures are estimates and do not satisfy generally accepted accounting practices (GAAP) rules.

quantitative analysis security analysis that uses objective statistical information to determine when to buy and sell securities.

quantitative fund a hedge fund that employs solely quantitative analysis and models in order to decide how to allocate and trade its assets and securities respectively.

quantitative model a model that utilizes numerical information to determine whether a security is attractive (see *Black box*).

redemption the sale of all of an investor's interests in a fund.

redemption fee this fee is often imposed by a hedge fund manager if the redemption occurs prior to the end of the first redemption period.

redemption notice period this refers to the official notice period that an investor must provide to the hedge fund manager before withdrawing the investment from the fund.

regulation D (Reg D) a Securities and Exchange Commission (SEC) regulation concerning private placement exemptions and thus allowing companies to raise capital through the sales of equity or the creation of debt, without registering any of these securities with the SEC.

repurchase agreement also known as repos or RPs, repurchase agreements occur when a seller sells a security for cash by agreeing to repurchase it at a premium at a later date.

rho a measurement of the rate of change in the price of a derivative relative to a change in the risk-free interest rate.

risk arbitrage a practice where investors bet on potential mergers or acquisitions of companies, by shorting the stock of the acquirer and going long the stock of the potential target, hoping that if the transaction takes place, the acquirer's stock will fall and the target company's stock will rise.

section 3(c)(1) a provision in the Investment Company Act of 1940 that permits hedge funds to have 100 investors, provided all investors are qualified purchasers and allows the exclusion of the funds from registration with the SEC.

section 3(c)(7) a provision in the Investment Company Act of 1940 that permits hedge funds to have more than 100 investors, provided all investors are purchasers and allows the exclusion of the funds from registration with the SEC.

sharpe ratio developed by Nobel Laureate William Sharpe, the ratio measures the reward of a portfolio's excess return relative to the volatility of the portfolio. It represents the absolute return less the risk-free interest rate divided by the standard deviation of returns.

short-sell short-selling is the practice of borrowing a stock, selling it at a high market price hoping that the market price will decrease and, thus, the stock can be repurchased at a lower price and returned to its original owner. The difference is then pocketed by the short-seller. Nowadays, it is possible to short-sell by utilizing options that enable the exerciser to sell options at a strike price which, if higher than the market price, will enable the short-seller to profit.

short-sell rule short position a transaction to sell shares of stock that the investor does not own. the short-sell rule was a regulation created by the Securities and Exchange Commission (SEC) that prohibited short sales from being placed on a downtick in the market price of the shares. In July 2007, this rule was changed, enabling short-sales of securities on any price tick in the market.

short position a transaction to sell shares of stock that the investor does not own.

standard deviation a measure of the dispersion of a group of numerical values from the mean. It is calculated by taking the difference between each number in the group and the arithmetic average, squaring them to give the variance, summing them, and taking the square root.

statistical arbitrage an opportunity for investors to profit from price mismatch between securities identified through the use of sophisticated mathematical modeling techniques. StatArb, as it is often abbreviated, involves very short holding periods and a large number of securities traded, as well as a powerful IT infrastructure.

style drift an expression used to describe manager behavior which consists of a divergence from the manager's initial investment style.

survivorship bias the tendency of mutual fund companies to drop their worst performing mutual funds, resulting in a better track record and a distortion of the data used to describe past performance.

systemic risk systemic risk is the risk presented by the market itself and impacts all securities encompassed in that particular market.

theta measures the rate of decrease in the value of an option as time passes.

traditional investments products whose performances are correlated with broad stock market or fixed-income markets.

treynor ratio measures returns earned in excess of those that could have been earned on a risk-free investment per unit of market risk. It is calculated by subtracting the average return of the risk-free rate from the average return of the portfolio and then dividing the answer by the beta of the portfolio.

vega a measure of how sensitive the price of an option is compared to a 1% change in implied volatility. It is the derivative of the option price with respect to the underlying asset.

VIX the ticker symbol for the Chicago Board Options Exchange Volatility Index, often used as a measure of the S&P 500 Index options.

Wilderhill Clean Energy Index an index used as a benchmark for investments in the alternative energy space.

Notes

Introduction

1. Bloomberg News, "BlackRock Inc. buys Barclays unit to become the world's largest money manager; manages $2.7 trillion." Friday, June 12, 2009. http://www.nydailynews.com/money/2009/06/12/2009-06-12_blackrock_inc_buys_barclays_unit_to_become_worlds_largest_money_manager_manages_.html.
2. Accredited Investors—http://www.sec.gov/answers/accred.htm.
3. Ibid.

Chapter 1 Hedge Fund Basics

1. Wall Street Journal, "Tiger Fund Has September Loss of $2.1 Billion," *Wall Street Journal*, September 17, 1998, C1.
2. These numbers were verified with Tiger Management's spokesman Fraser Seitel of Emerald Partners Communications Counselors on December 15, 1998.
3. The profit would be slightly less because there is some cost associated with the use of leverage.
4. Diana B. Henriques, "Fault Lines of Risk Appear As Market Hero Stumbles," *New York Times*, September 27, 1998, 1, 28.
5. This is the only firm to earn money on its investment. Many firms made a lot of money trading with Long-Term Capital as their broker.
6. Diana B. Henriques, "Fault Lines of Risk Appear As Market Hero Stumbles," the *New York Times*, September 27, 1998, 1, 28.
7. BarclayHedge, Ltd.—http://www.barclayhedge.com/research/indices/ghs/Hedge_Fund_Index.html.

8. http://www.independent.co.uk/news/business/news/wall-streets-golden-boy-paulson-loses-some-glister-1895962.html.
9. http://www.finalternatives.com/node/11381.
10. There is no one source for data on the hedge fund industry; there is only speculation since, unlike the U.S.-based mutual fund industry, there is no reporting requirement for hedge funds and as such there is no way of knowing just how many funds exist and how much money is truly under management.
11. Wyndham Robertson, "Hedge-Fund Miseries," *Fortune*, May 1971, 269.
12. Ibid.
13. An accredited investor is defined by the Securities and Exchange Commission as an individual or couple that has earned $200,000 or $300,000 respectively in the past two years and will do so in the next year, or has a net worth of a million dollars. A super-accredited investor is a person and/or a family that has net investable assets in excess of $5 million.
14. Bethany McLean, "Everybody's Going Hedge Funds," *Fortune*, June 8, 1998, 177–184.
15. Ibid.
16. Reprinted from the March 1949 issue of *Fortune* by special permission; copyright 1949, Time Inc.
17. John Thackray, "Whatever Happened to the Hedge Funds?" *Institutional Investor*, May 1977, 70–73.
18. Carol J. Loomis, "Hard Times Come to the Hedge Funds," *Fortune*, January 1970, 100–103, 134–138.

Chapter 2 How Hedge Funds Operate

1. Carol J. Loomis, "Hard Times Come to Hedge Funds," *Fortune*, January 1970, 100–103, 134–138.
2. *Wall Street Journal*, February 2, 1998.
3. Neither the Soros organization nor Mr. Niederhoffer would comment as to whether the funding came from the Soros organization. It is pure market and industry speculation.
4. It is the norm in the industry that the broker/marketer who brings investment dollars to the fund gets a piece of the fees that the dollars add to the fund's bottom line.

5. This comment is for illustration purposes only. It is not to imply that either fund manager farms money out to other managers.
6. James M. Clash, "Wretched Excess," *Forbes,* April 20, 1998, 478–480.
7. Michael Siconolfi, "Bond Market Still Punishes Hedge Fund and Investors," *Wall Street Journal,* October 5, 1998, page C1.
8. Carol J. Loomis, "Hard Times Come to the Hedge Funds," *Fortune,* January 1970, 100–103, 134–138.
9. Ibid.
10. Stephanie Strom, "Top Manager to Close Shop on Hedge Funds," the *New York Times,* October 12, 1995, D1.
11. Ibid.
12. I must make it clear that these numbers are used for illustration purposes only. It is impossible to confirm exactly how much money the Soros organization—or any other hedge fund for that matter—earns and receives for its efforts.
13. Most money managers meet and visit executives at companies they either are planning to invest in or already own.
14. Wall Street Journal, "Business Week Agrees to Settle Libel Suit Brought by Investor," *Wall Street Journal,* December 18, 1997, B6.

About the Author

Daniel Strachman is a financial expert with more than 15 years of Wall Street experience. He is nationally recognized as a strategist, futurist, and commentator on Wall Street, the economy, and investment strategy.

Daniel specializes in providing strategic advice and counsel to companies that want to expand and prosper in both good and bad economic times. His clients are a who's who of global investment firms and financial services companies.

Throughout his extensive career, Daniel has worked in institutional brokerage, money management, and mutual fund and hedge fund product development and marketing. He is an expert in all aspects of retail and institutional distribution for both traditional and alternative investment products and services.

Daniel is the author of seven books on investment strategy, the hedge fund industry, and investment management. His articles have appeared in the *Financial Times,* the *Boston Globe, Interview Magazine,* the *New York Post,* and *American Banker.* He blogs at www.hedgeanswers.com.

Daniel frequently appears in broadcast and print media. He is a former adjunct professor at New York University's School of Continuing Education and has lectured at the New York Society of Securities Analysts.

He is a graduate of Clark University.

Index